Canadian Living's best

CHICKEN

BY

Elizabeth Baird

AND

The Food Writers of Canadian Living Magazine
and The Canadian Living Test Kitchen

A MADISON PRESS BOOK
PRODUCED FOR
BALLANTINE BOOKS AND CANADIAN LIVING™

Ballantine Books
A Division of
Random House of
Canada Limited
1265 Aerowood Drive
Mississauga, Ontario
Canada
L4W 1B9

Canadian Living
Telemedia
Communications Inc.
50 Holly Street
Toronto, Ontario
Canada
M4S 3B3

Canadian Cataloguing in Publication Data

Chicken

(Canadian Living's best)
ISBN 0-345-39796-7

1. Cookery (Chicken).   I. Baird, Elizabeth.
II. Series.

TX750.5.C45C45 1994   641.6'65   C94-930274-0

™Canadian Living is a trade mark owned by
Telemedia Communications Inc.
and licensed by The Madison Press Limited.
All trade mark rights, registered or unregistered,
are reserved worldwide.

**Produced by
Madison Press Books
40 Madison Avenue
Toronto, Ontario
Canada
M5R 2S1**

Printed in Canada

Contents

Introduction

What do most cooks love about chicken?

The answer we often hear from our readers is — "It's versatile!" Open a dictionary and "versatile" is defined as "turning easily."

And that's exactly what chicken does. It turns with delicious ease and grace from one flavor to another — mushroom and mustard one day, lemony ginger the next, basil and tomatoes, too. Orange, cumin or honey can follow, and no one will ever be bored when chicken is the star ingredient.

Just as effortlessly, chicken does global spins, from Cajun to Indian curry, gutsy Southwestern to fiery Jamaican, with pauses around Europe and South America. And we shouldn't forget all the Pacific Rim nations whose cuisines we have grown to love — China, Thailand and Japan. Each country contributes its own unique and likeable blend of aromas and tastes.

Chicken is so adaptable it can be cooked almost every existing way. In the summer, chicken sizzling on the barbecue lures family and friends for alfresco suppers. Come the winter, the aroma of chicken roasting and crisping in the oven brings on the proverbial mouth-watering-in-anticipation experience. Chicken simmers into one wonderful soup, sautés into elegant dinners, and stews gloriously under a golden pot-pie crust.

You can dress chicken up for company, dress it down for quick weeknight meals, cook it whole or in pieces, white or dark, bone-in, boneless, hot or cold. And it's perfect for lunch, dinner or supper with just about any side dish. Chicken does it all and does it so well that you will never stop trying new dishes. And that's where *Canadian Living's Best Chicken* takes its cue, offering you more than 100 new and delicious ways to flavor and savor chicken.

Elizabeth Baird

Favorites For Every Occasion

Chicken is a star in the kitchen — whether you need it fast and no-fuss for weekday suppers, or have the time to jazz it up into an impressive special-occasion dish.

Chicken Breasts with Mushroom Sauce ▶

Bathed in a new-style low-fat creamy sauce, nobbled with mushrooms and fresh with onions, chicken proves once again that it's an incredibly versatile and economical main dish.

1/4 cup	all-purpose flour	50 mL
2 tbsp	light sour cream	25 mL
4 tsp	Dijon mustard	20 mL
1 cup	chicken stock	250 mL
4	boneless skinless chicken breasts	4
Pinch	each dried thyme, salt and pepper	Pinch
1 tbsp	butter	15 mL
1-1/2 cups	quartered mushrooms	375 mL
3	green onions, cut into 1-inch (2.5 cm) pieces	3
	Chopped fresh parsley	

● Whisk together 2 tsp (10 mL) of the flour, sour cream, mustard and 2 tbsp (25 mL) of the chicken stock; set aside.

● Sprinkle one side of chicken with thyme, salt and pepper; dredge in remaining flour. In large nonstick skillet, melt butter over medium-low heat until foaming. Cook chicken for about 5 minutes on each side or until no longer pink inside. Remove to warmed serving platter; cover and keep warm.

● Add mushrooms to skillet; cook, stirring, for 3 minutes. Add remaining chicken stock; increase heat to high and boil for 3 minutes. Whisk in sour cream mixture; add onions. Cook, stirring, for about 3 minutes or until thickened. Pour over chicken. Garnish with parsley. Makes 4 servings.

VARIATION

APPLE CARAWAY CHICKEN: Substitute crushed caraway seeds for thyme. Replace 1/2 cup (125 mL) of the stock with apple juice. Replace onions with 1 large diced (unpeeled) tart apple. Decrease mustard to 1 tbsp (15 mL) and add along with 2 tsp (10 mL) cider vinegar.

HOW TO BONE A CHICKEN BREAST

1 With fingers, pull off skin from chicken; trim any fat on edges of meat. Place chicken on cutting board, bone side down.

2 Using tip of sharp knife, make shallow cut along ridge of breastbone between meat and bone.

3 Holding knife flat against bone and working with short strokes, cut between meat and bone to within 1/4 inch (5 mm) of other edge, lifting meat away with fingers.

4 Open breast out flat; cut meat neatly away from edge of bone. Reserve bones to make stock (recipe, p.44).

Chunky Chicken Pasta ▼

Bite-size chunks of chicken in a quick tomato and vegetable mixture make an easy Monday-to-Friday supper. Any short pasta such as rotini or rigatoni can replace the macaroni.

1-1/2 cups	macaroni	375 mL
3 cups	chopped broccoli florets	750 mL
4	boneless skinless chicken breasts	4
2 tbsp	olive oil	25 mL
1	can (19 oz/540 mL) tomatoes	1
6	green onions, chopped	6
1/2 cup	chopped oil-packed sun-dried tomatoes (about 3 oz/90 g)	125 mL
2 tbsp	tomato paste	25 mL
1 tsp	dried oregano	5 mL
1/4 tsp	pepper	1 mL
1/4 cup	freshly grated Parmesan cheese	50 mL

● In large pot of boiling salted water, cook macaroni for 8 to 10 minutes or until tender but firm. Add broccoli; cook for 1 minute. Drain.

● Meanwhile, cut chicken into bite-size chunks. In large skillet or wok, heat oil over high heat; cook chicken, stirring occasionally, for 3 to 4 minutes or until browned.

● Chop or mash tomatoes, reserving juice; add to pan along with juice. Add onions, sun-dried tomatoes, tomato paste, oregano and pepper; reduce heat to medium and simmer for about 2 minutes or until chicken is no longer pink inside.

● Stir in macaroni mixture; toss together until well coated. Sprinkle with Parmesan. Makes 4 servings.

Orange Hoisin Chicken Breasts

1/3 cup	hoisin sauce	75 mL
1 tsp	grated orange rind	5 mL
1/3 cup	orange juice	75 mL
1 tbsp	soy sauce	15 mL
3	cloves garlic, minced	3
1 tbsp	minced gingerroot	15 mL
1 tsp	Chinese five-spice powder (optional)	5 mL
Dash	hot pepper sauce	Dash
8	chicken breasts	8
1 tbsp	liquid honey	15 mL

● In large bowl, stir together hoisin sauce, orange rind and juice, soy sauce, garlic, ginger, Chinese five-spice powder (if using) and hot pepper sauce.

● Add chicken, turning to coat evenly. Cover and marinate at room temperature for 30 minutes or in refrigerator for up to 4 hours. Remove from refrigerator 30 minutes before cooking.

● Reserving marinade, arrange chicken, skin side up, in single layer in shallow roasting pan. Roast in 375°F (190°C) oven for 20 minutes. Stir honey into marinade and brush over chicken; roast, brushing once with pan juices, for about 20 minutes longer or until chicken is no longer pink inside. Makes 8 servings.

These burnished chicken breasts are an excellent focus for a no-fuss dinner party. Rice and steamed broccoli tossed with toasted sesame seeds are excellent accompaniments and are just as easy to prepare.

ONE BREAST OR TWO?
Throughout this book, any chicken breast called for in a recipe is a single, not a double, breast.

Skillet Chicken and Ham

2 tbsp	all-purpose flour	25 mL
Pinch	each paprika and pepper	Pinch
4	boneless skinless chicken breasts	4
2 tbsp	olive oil	25 mL
1/4 lb	Black Forest ham, cubed	125 g
1	sweet red pepper, chopped	1
1	onion, chopped	1
2	cloves garlic, minced	2
1 cup	chopped canned tomatoes	250 mL
Pinch	hot pepper flakes	Pinch
	Salt	
	Chopped fresh parsley or olives	

● In shallow dish, combine flour, paprika and pepper; dredge chicken in mixture.

● In large skillet, heat oil over medium-high heat; cook chicken for 3 minutes. Turn and cook for 1 minute; remove from skillet and set aside.

● Add ham to skillet; stir until lightly browned. Add red pepper, onion and garlic; cook for 3 minutes or until onion is softened.

● Stir in tomatoes, hot pepper flakes, and salt to taste. Return chicken to skillet (less-cooked side down); reduce heat and simmer for 5 to 6 minutes or until no longer pink inside. Sprinkle with parsley. Makes 4 servings.

Chicken breasts simmer in a colorful Spanish-inspired sauce you can mop up with thick slices of crusty bread. A green salad tangy with orange and onion slices is perfect as a side dish.

TIP: To dredge chicken or other meat, fish or vegetables, place individual pieces of the food in the flour mixture, turning to coat evenly on all sides. Lift, shaking to remove excess. Or, place flour mixture in paper bag and shake individual pieces of food. Remove and shake off excess.

Chicken Fajitas

Make-your-own fajitas are sure to be a suppertime hit. Have warmed tortillas and bowls of fresh coriander, lettuce and cheese ready, then bring the fast-fry chicken mixture to the table and let everyone get filling, rolling and eating.

4	boneless skinless chicken breasts	4
5	onions	5
2	sweet green or red peppers	2
2 tbsp	vegetable oil	25 mL
1 tsp	ground coriander seeds	5 mL
1/2 tsp	salt	2 mL
1/4 tsp	hot pepper flakes	1 mL
12	flour tortillas, warmed	12
1 cup	each chopped fresh coriander, chopped lettuce and shredded Cheddar cheese	250 mL

● Cut chicken into strips. Slice onions and separate into rings. Seed and cut green peppers into strips.

● In large skillet, heat oil over high heat; brown chicken for 2 minutes. Add onions, green peppers, ground coriander, salt and hot pepper flakes; cook for 4 minutes or until chicken is no longer pink inside.

● Spoon chicken mixture onto center of each tortilla; sprinkle with fresh coriander, lettuce and cheese. Roll up. Makes 6 servings.

Basil Chicken Stir-Fry

This chunky stir-fry is delicious over soft polenta (recipe, p. 33), mashed sweet potatoes or a short pasta such as penne.

4	boneless skinless chicken breasts	4
3	sweet red peppers	3
3	sweet yellow peppers	3
1	red onion	1
1/4 cup	olive oil	50 mL
2	cloves garlic, minced	2
1	hot banana pepper, diced (optional)	1
1 tsp	chopped fresh rosemary (or 1/4 tsp/1 mL dried)	5 mL
1/2 cup	dry white wine or chicken stock	125 mL
1 tsp	Dijon mustard	5 mL
1/2 tsp	each salt and pepper	2 mL
1/4 cup	chopped fresh basil	50 mL

● Cut chicken and sweet peppers into 1-inch (2.5 cm) pieces. Cut onion into 1/2-inch (1 cm) chunks.

● In skillet, heat half of the oil over medium-high heat; stir-fry chicken for 5 minutes or until lightly browned. Remove from skillet; set aside.

● Wipe out skillet and add remaining oil; cook onion and garlic for about 3 minutes or until softened. Add sweet peppers, hot banana pepper (if using) and rosemary; cook, stirring occasionally, for 10 minutes. Add wine, mustard, salt and pepper; cook, stirring occasionally, for 5 minutes.

● Return chicken to skillet; cook for 5 minutes or until no longer pink inside. Stir in basil. Makes 4 servings.

TIP: Wear rubber gloves when handling hot peppers. Choose the bulkier all-purpose gloves that should be scrubbed after use or disposable skin-tight vinyl ones available in drugstores. The burning component of peppers can seriously irritate hands and any other parts of the body it touches. Avoid touching your body even with the gloves.

Harvest Chicken ▲

2 tbsp	olive oil	25 mL
3	cloves garlic, minced	3
1	onion, chopped	1
Pinch	hot pepper flakes	Pinch
2 cups	cubed zucchini	500 mL
1 cup	diced sweet red pepper	250 mL
1/3 cup	shredded mozzarella cheese	75 mL
1 tbsp	chopped fresh basil (or 1 tsp/5 mL dried)	15 mL
1/2 tsp	salt	2 mL
1/4 tsp	pepper	1 mL
2	whole boneless chicken breasts	2
	Fresh basil leaves	

● In large ovenproof skillet, heat half of the oil over medium heat; cook garlic, onion and hot pepper flakes for 3 minutes or until onion is softened.

● Add zucchini and red pepper; cook, stirring, for 3 minutes. Remove from heat; stir in cheese, chopped basil, salt and pepper. Let cool slightly.

● Using fingers, gently loosen skin from thick end of chicken breasts to form pocket, leaving skin attached at edges. Stuff half of the vegetable mixture into each pocket, patting gently to flatten slightly. Secure skin at edges with toothpicks.

● In same skillet, heat remaining oil over medium heat; cook chicken, skin side down, for about 3 minutes or until golden brown.

● Turn skin side up; bake in 375°F (190°C) oven for about 30 minutes or until chicken is no longer pink inside. Halve breasts vertically. Garnish with basil leaves. Makes 4 servings.

A *toss of summer vegetables and fresh basil roasted under the skin of double chicken breasts adds an impressive party touch to any meal.*

Sweet Pepper-Stuffed Chicken Breasts ◄

1	each sweet red, green and yellow pepper	1
1 tbsp	butter	15 mL
3/4 tsp	each salt and pepper	4 mL
1/2 tsp	dried thyme	2 mL
4	boneless chicken breasts	4
1/3 cup	chicken stock or white wine	75 mL
1 tsp	Dijon mustard	5 mL

● Remove one-quarter of each sweet pepper; cut into decorative shapes and set aside. Cut remaining sweet peppers into thin strips.

● In nonstick skillet, melt butter over medium heat; cook sweet pepper strips and 1/4 tsp (1 mL) each of the salt, pepper and thyme, stirring, for 3 minutes. Set aside.

● Pat chicken dry. Place, skin side up, between 2 sheets of waxed paper; pound lightly to 1/4-inch (5 mm) thickness.

● Turn chicken over; sprinkle skinless sides with 1/4 tsp (1 mL) each of the salt and pepper. Place pepper strips crosswise on short end of each breast; roll up and secure with toothpicks. Sprinkle with remaining salt, pepper and thyme.

● In same skillet, brown chicken lightly on all sides. Transfer to baking sheet; bake in 375°F (190°C) oven for 10 to 15 minutes or until chicken is no longer pink inside.

● Meanwhile, in skillet, bring chicken stock to boil, stirring to scrape up brown bits. Stir in mustard; cook, stirring, over medium heat for about 2 minutes or until slightly reduced. Spoon over chicken. Garnish with sweet pepper cutouts. Makes 4 servings.

Beautiful enough for special spring dinners, these chicken breasts are bursting with the fresh flavors of simple ingredients. Double the recipe if you have extra guests.

Pan-Fried Chicken with Red Pepper Purée

3 tbsp	all-purpose flour	50 mL
1/2 tsp	each salt, pepper and dried thyme	2 mL
4	boneless skinless chicken breasts	4
3 tbsp	vegetable oil	50 mL
1	sweet red pepper, sliced	1
1	clove garlic, minced	1
1/2 cup	chicken stock	125 mL
1 tsp	Dijon mustard	5 mL

● In shallow dish, combine flour, salt, pepper and thyme; lightly dredge chicken in mixture. Set aside.

● In skillet, heat 1 tbsp (15 mL) of the oil over medium heat; cook red pepper and garlic, stirring occasionally, for 5 minutes or until softened. Transfer to blender. Add stock and mustard; purée until smooth.

● In skillet, heat remaining oil over medium heat; cook chicken, turning once, for 10 to 15 minutes or until no longer pink inside. Remove from skillet; keep warm.

● Drain off any fat from skillet; add purée and heat through, scraping up brown bits from bottom of pan. Divide purée among plates; top with chicken. Makes 4 servings.

Chicken breasts are crisp and golden on a pool of puréed sweet red pepper. Fried, yes, but not fatty.

Chicken and Orange Stir-Fry

Perfect for busy households, the Orange Stir-Fry Sauce can be made ahead and sauces two great wokfulls. For a change of taste, replace the orange juice with pineapple juice.

4	boneless skinless chicken breasts	4
2 tbsp	olive oil	25 mL
2	cloves garlic, minced	2
1 tbsp	chopped gingerroot	15 mL
2 cups	broccoli florets	500 mL
1	sweet red pepper, julienned	1
2	small carrots, thinly sliced on diagonal	2
Half	red onion, thinly sliced	Half
1 cup	sliced mushrooms	250 mL
3/4 cup	Orange Stir-Fry Sauce (recipe follows)	175 mL
1/4 cup	chopped fresh coriander	50 mL

● Slice chicken into 1/4-inch (5 mm) thick strips.

● In wok or large skillet, heat 1 tbsp (15 mL) of the oil over high heat; stir-fry chicken, in batches if necessary, for about 5 minutes or until no longer pink inside. Transfer to plate.

● Add remaining oil to skillet; stir-fry garlic and ginger for 30 seconds. Add broccoli, red pepper and carrots; stir-fry for 1 minute. Add onion and mushrooms; stir-fry for 30 seconds.

● Pour in half of the Orange Stir-Fry Sauce; cover and steam for 2 minutes or until broccoli is tender-crisp.

● Return chicken to wok; push contents to side of pan. Pour remaining sauce into center of wok; cook, stirring, for 2 minutes or until thickened. Stir chicken and vegetables back into sauce until glazed and coated. Sprinkle with coriander. Makes 4 servings.

ORANGE STIR-FRY SAUCE		
1 tsp	orange rind	5 mL
3/4 cup	each orange juice and hoisin sauce	175 mL
1/4 cup	rice wine vinegar	50 mL
1/4 cup	chicken stock or water	50 mL
2 tbsp	soy sauce	25 mL
1/4 cup	cornstarch	50 mL

● In small saucepan, combine orange rind and juice, hoisin sauce, vinegar, chicken stock, soy sauce and cornstarch; bring to boil. Reduce heat and simmer for 15 minutes. *(Sauce can be refrigerated in airtight container for up to 1 week.)* Makes 1-1/2 cups (375 mL).

Sesame Glazed Chicken

Here's an easy Oriental chicken to serve with steamed asparagus and wide Chinese wheat noodles or rice.

4	chicken legs	4
1/4 cup	oyster sauce	50 mL
4 tsp	liquid honey	20 mL
2 tsp	Dijon mustard	10 mL
1/2 tsp	sesame oil	2 mL
Pinch	pepper	Pinch
2 tbsp	sesame seeds	25 mL
1	green onion, chopped	1

● Remove skin from chicken; separate legs at joint. Arrange on greased baking sheet. Combine oyster sauce, honey, mustard, sesame oil and pepper; brush over chicken. Sprinkle with sesame seeds.

● Bake in 375°F (190°C) oven for 40 minutes or until juices run clear when chicken is pierced. Remove to warmed platter; sprinkle with green onion. Makes 4 servings.

TIP: Chinese grocery stores are the most reliable and inexpensive source of fresh noodles and Oriental ingredients such as oyster sauce and sesame oil.

THAWING CHICKEN

- **In refrigerator:** 5 hours per pound (500 g).
- **In cold water**: thaw in sealed packages, changing water frequently. Allow

1 hour per pound (500 g).
- **In microwave:** thaw on defrost (50% setting), separating and turning pieces as chicken thaws. Allow

5 minutes per pound (500 g).
- Once thawed, refrigerate chicken and cook within 2 days. Do not refreeze thawed chicken.

- NEVER THAW CHICKEN AT ROOM TEMPERATURE.

Crispy Chicken Legs ▼

4	chicken legs	4
1/2 cup	plain low-fat yogurt	125 mL
1/2 tsp	dried thyme	2 mL
1/4 tsp	each salt and pepper	1 mL
Pinch	cayenne pepper	Pinch
1-1/2 cups	corn flakes, finely crushed	375 mL
1/4 cup	freshly grated Parmesan Cheese	50 mL

- Remove skin from chicken. In shallow dish, mix together yogurt, thyme, salt, pepper and cayenne. In another shallow dish, combine corn flakes and Parmesan.

- Roll chicken in yogurt mixture to coat all over; roll in crumb mixture. Bake on lightly greased baking sheet in 350°F (180°C) oven for 45 minutes or until crispy and juices run clear when chicken is pierced. Makes 4 servings.

Instead of the skin and all its fat, here's a golden crunchy coating that does the job of sealing in the juices — and tastes wonderful, too.

New Chicken Cacciatore ▲

Removing the skin before browning chicken eliminates about 7 grams of fat per leg. And you'll never miss the skin when the legs are cooked in this comfy tomato, mushroom and vegetable sauce.

4	chicken legs	4
1 tbsp	olive oil	15 mL
2	onions, chopped	2
2	carrots, chopped	2
2-1/2 cups	halved mushrooms (about 1/2 lb/250 g)	625 mL
2	cloves garlic, minced	2
1	bay leaf	1
1 tsp	dried basil	5 mL
1/2 tsp	each dried oregano and thyme	2 mL
1	can (19 oz/540 mL) tomatoes	1
1	can (14 oz/398 mL) tomato sauce	1
	Salt and pepper	
12 oz	spaghetti	375 g
	Chopped fresh parsley	

● Remove skin from chicken; separate legs at joint. In large nonstick skillet, heat oil over medium-high heat; add chicken and cook, turning often, for 7 to 10 minutes or until browned all over. Remove and set aside.

● Reduce heat to medium. Add onions, carrots, mushrooms, garlic, bay leaf, basil, oregano and thyme; cook, stirring often, for 3 minutes. Add tomatoes, breaking up with spoon; add tomato sauce.

● Return chicken to skillet; bring sauce to boil. Reduce heat and simmer, uncovered and stirring occasionally, for 30 to 40 minutes or until juices run clear when chicken is pierced and sauce is slightly thickened. Season with salt and pepper to taste. Discard bay leaf.

● Meanwhile, in large pot of boiling salted water, cook spaghetti until tender but firm; drain. Serve chicken over spaghetti; garnish with parsley. Makes 4 servings.

Golden Oven-Fried Chicken

1 tbsp	each butter and vegetable oil	15 mL
1-1/4 cups	dry bread crumbs	300 mL
1 tbsp	paprika	15 mL
1-1/2 tsp	each dried marjoram, dry mustard and pepper	7 mL
3/4 tsp	salt	4 mL
2	cloves garlic, minced	2
1/2 cup	milk	125 mL
8	chicken legs	8

● In large rimmed baking sheet, melt butter with oil in 375°F (190°C) oven, tilting pan to coat evenly.

● Meanwhile, in shallow dish, combine bread crumbs, paprika, marjoram, mustard, pepper, salt and garlic. Pour milk into another dish.

● Separate chicken legs at joint. Dip chicken into crumb mixture, then into milk; dip again into crumb mixture to coat well. Arrange, meaty side down and without touching, on baking sheet.

● Bake for 20 minutes; turn and bake for 20 to 25 minutes longer or until juices run clear when chicken is pierced. Makes 8 servings.

*W*hy deep-fry when baking coated chicken in the oven makes it just as crisp and succulent? This oven-fried chicken is especially good in summer served hot with corn on the cob and new potatoes, or chilled and packed in a cooler for a relaxing picnic in the park.

Herbed Chicken Thighs

8	chicken thighs	8
1	clove garlic, minced	1
1/4 cup	red wine vinegar	50 mL
1 tbsp	olive oil	15 mL
1 tsp	each dried thyme and oregano	5 mL
1/4 tsp	hot pepper sauce	1 mL
Pinch	paprika	Pinch

● Remove skin from chicken if desired; place in lightly greased 11- x 7-inch (2 L) baking dish.

● Combine garlic, vinegar, oil, thyme, oregano, hot pepper sauce and paprika; spoon over chicken. Cover and marinate in refrigerator, turning occasionally, for at least 15 minutes or up to 8 hours. Let stand at room temperature for 30 minutes.

● Bake in 375°F (190°C) oven, basting halfway through, for 30 to 35 minutes or until juices run clear when chicken is pierced. If skin is left on, broil for 2 to 3 minutes or until crisped. Skim off fat from pan juices; serve juices with chicken. Makes 4 servings.

A quick marinade livens up chicken and creates delicious pan juices to serve over the pieces. To round out this menu, start potatoes and butternut squash in the oven before baking the chicken and serve with a broccoli salad.

FLAVORING WITH HERBS

Herbs have earned much more room in our spice drawers and greater plate space on our tables. Fresh, they add lively notes of flavor to dishes; dried, they offer year-round echos of summer.

● When using fresh herbs, use two or three times the amount you would use of dried. When using dried herbs, avoid powdered or ground ones, choosing crumbled or crushed herb leaves instead.

● Some high-quality dried herbs are much stronger in flavor than home-dried and less expensive commercial dried herbs. So a word of caution whenever you feel lavish with herbs. This is especially true of some of the stronger herbs such as thyme, sage and summer savory.

● Don't let dried herbs outstay their welcome. Any that have resided longer than six months in your cupboard should be tasted — and discarded if they've lost their zip.

Chicken with Lemon and Garlic

Choose juicy thin-skinned lemons for this dish from the Lebanese community in Prince Edward Island. In summer, grill the chicken for 30 to 40 minutes or until crisp and golden, basting it often with the garlicky lemon marinade.

4 lb	chicken pieces	1.8 kg
5	cloves garlic	5
2 tsp	salt	10 mL
1 cup	lemon juice	250 mL
1/4 cup	vegetable oil	50 mL
1 tbsp	cinnamon	15 mL
2 tsp	paprika	10 mL
1 tsp	black pepper	5 mL
1/4 tsp	cayenne pepper	1 mL

● Trim fat from chicken; cut into serving-size pieces, skinning if desired.

● Crush garlic with salt until pastelike; combine in large bowl with lemon juice, oil, cinnamon, paprika, and black and cayenne peppers. Add chicken and turn to coat; cover and marinate in refrigerator for at least 1 hour or up to 8 hours. Let stand at room temperature for 30 minutes.

● Transfer chicken and marinade to shallow baking dish; bake in 375°F (190°C) oven, basting often and turning once, for 45 minutes or until browned and juices run clear when chicken is pierced. Makes 8 servings.

Maple Chicken with Sausages ▶

When the occasion calls for comfort food for a crowd, this sausage and chicken combo napped with maple hits the spot. For a smaller gathering, simply cut back on quantities.

1/2 cup	all-purpose flour	125 mL
1 tsp	salt	5 mL
1/4 tsp	pepper	1 mL
4-1/2 lb	chicken pieces	2 kg
1 lb	small sausages	500 g
1	Spanish onion, sliced	1
1 tbsp	vegetable oil	15 mL
1/2 cup	maple syrup	125 mL

● In shallow dish, combine flour, salt and pepper; dredge chicken in mixture and set aside.

● Heat large skillet over medium-high heat; cook sausages for about 3 minutes or until lightly browned but not cooked completely. Remove and set aside.

● Separate onion into rings and add to skillet along with 3 tbsp (50 mL) water; cook for 5 minutes or until golden. Remove and set aside.

● Add oil to skillet; brown chicken, in batches, for about 5 minutes per side. Arrange in single layer in large roasting pan; top with sausages and onion.

● Drain fat from skillet; pour in 1/2 cup (125 mL) water, stirring to scrape up brown bits from bottom of pan. Stir in maple syrup; pour over chicken.

● Bake, uncovered, in 350°F (180°C) oven, basting occasionally, for 45 minutes or until tender and juices run clear when chicken is pierced. Skim fat from sauce; pass sauce separately. Makes 8 to 10 servings.

Country-French Chicken Loaf

Apple contributes moisture and sweetness to this chicken loaf. Extra applesauce, potatoes mashed with garlic and crunchy green beans complete this comfy meal for family or friends.

2 tbsp	butter	25 mL
1 cup	minced onion	250 mL
2	diced (unpeeled) Golden Delicious apples	2
2	cloves garlic, minced	2
1/2 tsp	dried tarragon	2 mL
1/4 tsp	dried savory	1 mL
2/3 cup	fresh bread crumbs	150 mL
2	eggs, beaten	2
1 tbsp	grated lemon rind	15 mL
2	green onions, chopped	2
1 tsp	salt	5 mL
1/2 tsp	pepper	2 mL
1 1/2 lb	ground chicken	750 g
	TOPPING	
1/2 cup	applesauce	125 mL
2 tbsp	dry bread crumbs	25 mL
1 tbsp	packed brown sugar	15 mL

● In large skillet, melt butter over medium heat; cook onion, apples and garlic, stirring occasionally, for 10 minutes or until golden. Add tarragon and savory; cook for 1 minute. Let cool for 10 minutes.

● In bowl, combine apple mixture, bread crumbs, eggs, lemon rind, green onions, salt and pepper; mix in chicken. Lightly pack into greased 9- x 5-inch (2 L) loaf pan, smoothing top.

● TOPPING: Spread loaf with applesauce; sprinkle with bread crumbs and brown sugar. Bake in 350°F (180°C) oven for 1 1/4 hours or until meat thermometer registers 185°F (85°C).

● Broil 6 inches (15 cm) from heat for 3 minutes or until golden. Let stand for 10 minutes before slicing. Makes 6 servings.

Quick Chicken Burritos

The easy-to-like Mexican flavors of cumin, oregano and chili — plus the increased availability of flour tortillas — have made dishes such as burritos and quesadillas popular fast food at home.

1 tbsp	vegetable oil	15 mL
1 lb	ground chicken	500 g
2	cloves garlic, minced	2
1	onion, chopped	1
1	small sweet red pepper, chopped	1
1	small zucchini, chopped	1
1 tsp	chili powder	5 mL
3/4 tsp	each dried oregano and ground cumin	4 mL
1	can (19 oz/540 mL) stewed tomatoes	1
	Salt and pepper	
8	flour tortillas	8
1 cup	shredded Monterey Jack or brick cheese	250 mL

● In large skillet, heat oil over medium-high heat. Add chicken, garlic, onion, red pepper, zucchini, half of the chili powder and 1/2 tsp (2 mL) each of the oregano and cumin; cook, stirring often, for 5 minutes or until chicken is no longer pink.

● Reserving tomatoes, drain juice into chicken mixture; bring to boil. Reduce heat and simmer for 5 minutes or until most of the liquid has evaporated. Season with salt and pepper to taste.

● Spoon chicken filling down center of each tortilla; sprinkle with half of the cheese. Roll up to enclose filling; arrange with sides touching on greased rimmed baking sheet.

● Add remaining chili powder, oregano and cumin to tomatoes; break up any large chunks. Spoon down center of each burrito; sprinkle with remaining cheese. Bake in 400°F (200°C) oven for 10 to 15 minutes or until heated through. Makes 4 servings.

Coriander Patties

1	egg	1
1 lb	ground chicken	500 g
1/2 cup	dry bread crumbs	125 mL
1/4 cup	finely chopped onion	50 mL
1/4 cup	chopped fresh coriander	50 mL
1 tsp	grated lemon rind	5 mL
1/2 tsp	salt	2 mL
1/4 tsp	pepper	1 mL
1 tbsp	vegetable oil	15 mL

● In large bowl, beat egg; mix in chicken, bread crumbs, onion, coriander, lemon rind, salt and pepper. Form into patties.

● In large nonstick skillet, heat oil over medium heat; cook patties for 5 to 6 minutes on each side or until golden brown on outside and no longer pink inside. Makes 4 servings.

In summer, grill these patties to slip into toasted kaisers along with sliced cucumbers and alfalfa sprouts. When it's too cold for grilling, pan-fry them and serve with ginger-glazed carrots and steamed rice tossed with green onions.

Chicken Burgers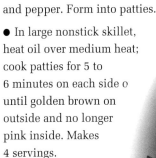

1	egg	1
1 lb	ground chicken	500 g
2/3 cup	dry bread crumbs	150 mL
1/2 cup	chopped green onions	125 mL
2 tbsp	chopped fresh parsley	25 mL
1 tbsp	freshly grated Parmesan cheese	15 mL
2 tsp	dry mustard	10 mL
1/2 tsp	salt	2 mL
1/4 tsp	pepper	1 mL
1 tbsp	vegetable oil	15 mL

While these well-seasoned burgers are in the skillet, steam a selection of vegetables — asparagus, patty-pan squash, small tender carrots and new potatoes are ideal choices. Chicken Burgers can also be cooked on greased grill for about 6 minutes per side. Then sandwich in toasted buns and add your favorite toppings.

● In large bowl, beat egg; mix in chicken, bread crumbs, onions, parsley, Parmesan cheese, mustard, salt and pepper. Form into patties.

● In large nonstick skillet, heat oil over medium heat; cook patties for 5 to 6 minutes on each side o until golden brown on outside and no longer pink inside. Makes 4 servings.

Light and Easy Chicken Chili

This recipe makes 8 cups (2 L) chili, enough to freeze for quick last-minute suppers in a bowl — or to enjoy in tacos, salad or quesadillas (see next page).

1 tbsp	vegetable oil	15 mL
2	onions	2
2	cloves garlic, minced	2
1 lb	ground chicken	500 g
1 cup	each chopped carrot and celery	250 mL
1	sweet red or green pepper, chopped	1
2 tbsp	chili powder	25 mL
1 tsp	ground cumin	5 mL
3/4 tsp	dried oregano	4 mL
1/2 tsp	salt	2 mL
1/4 tsp	each hot pepper flakes and pepper	1 mL
1	can (28 oz/796 mL) tomatoes, chopped	1
1	can (19 oz/540 mL) red kidney beans, drained and rinsed	1
1	can (19 oz/540 mL) chick-peas, drained and rinsed	1
1/4 cup	chopped fresh parsley	50 mL

● In large heavy saucepan or Dutch oven, heat oil over medium heat; cook onions and garlic, stirring, for about 5 minutes or until softened.

● Add chicken; cook, stirring, for about 7 minutes or until no longer pink. Add carrot, celery, red pepper, chili powder, cumin, oregano, salt, hot pepper flakes and pepper; cook, stirring, for 1 minute.

● Pour in tomatoes and kidney beans; bring to boil. Reduce heat, cover and simmer for 15 minutes. Add chick-peas; simmer for 15 minutes. Garnish with parsley. Makes 4 to 6 servings.

White Chicken Chili

White beans and chicken give new taste and color to a Monday-to-Friday favorite. A choice of toppings rounds out a hearty meal-in-a-bowl. For convenience, substitute one 19-ounce (540 mL) can white beans, drained and rinsed.

1 tbsp	vegetable oil	15 mL
2	onions, chopped	2
3	cloves garlic, minced	3
1-1/4 lb	boneless skinless chicken, cubed	625 g
2 tsp	ground cumin	10 mL
1 tsp	dried oregano	5 mL
Pinch	each salt and cayenne pepper	Pinch
1	can (4 oz/114 mL) mild green chilies, drained (or 1 large sweet green pepper, chopped)	1
1-1/2 cups	chicken stock	375 mL
2 cups	cooked white beans	500 mL
1/4 cup	diced sweet red pepper or pimiento	50 mL
	GARNISH	
1/4 cup	chopped fresh coriander or parsley	50 mL
1/4 cup	shredded Cheddar cheese	50 mL
1/4 cup	slivered black olives	50 mL
1/4 cup	chopped tomatoes	50 mL
1/4 cup	light sour cream	50 mL

● In Dutch oven, heat half of the oil over medium heat; cook onions and garlic for 4 minutes or until softened. Remove and set aside.

● Add remaining oil to pan; increase heat to medium-high and cook chicken, in batches, until light golden. Add onion mixture, cumin, oregano, salt and cayenne; cook, stirring, for 2 minutes.

● Add green chilies and chicken stock; bring to boil. Reduce heat and simmer, covered, for 15 minutes or until chicken is no longer pink inside. Add beans and red pepper; heat through. Taste and adjust seasoning.

● Garnish each serving with coriander, Cheddar, olives, tomatoes and sour cream. Makes 4 servings.

CHICKEN CHILI THREE WAYS

Here are three family-pleasing ways to enjoy Light and Easy Chicken Chili.

CHILI TACOS

8	taco shells	8
2 cups	chicken chili, heated	500 mL
4 cups	shredded lettuce	1 L
1 cup	sour cream	250 mL
1 cup	shredded Monterey Jack cheese	250 mL
1/2 cup	chunky salsa	125 mL

● Fill each taco shell with 1/4 cup (50 mL) chili. Top with lettuce, sour cream, cheese and salsa. Makes 4 servings.

CHILI TACO SALAD ▲

4 cups	tortilla chips	1 L
4 cups	chicken chili, heated	1 L
4 cups	shredded lettuce	1 L
2 cups	chopped fresh tomatoes	500 mL
1 cup	sour cream	250 mL
1 cup	shredded Monterey Jack cheese	250 mL
1/2 cup	chopped black olives	125 mL
1/2 cup	chopped jalapeño peppers	125 mL
12	mini corn cobs (optional)	12

● Divide chips evenly among four plates. Top each with 1 cup (250 mL) chili, then lettuce, tomatoes, sour cream, cheese, olives, jalapeño peppers, and corn (if using). Makes 4 servings.

CHILI CHEESE QUESADILLAS

8	8-inch (20 cm) flour tortillas	8
8 cups	chicken chili	2 L
2-2/3 cups	shredded Monterey Jack cheese	650 mL

● Lay tortillas flat on work surface. Spread each with 1 cup (250 mL) chili; sprinkle with 1/3 cup (75 mL) cheese and fold in half. Bake on baking sheet in 350°F (180°C) oven for about 7 minutes or until heated through and cheese has melted. Makes 4 servings.

One-Dish Suppers

Chicken simmers to slow and flavorful perfection in a host of stews, casseroles, curries and jambalayas that will have everyone coming back for seconds.

Southwestern Chicken Stew ▶

Chicken thighs make a great budget-minded stew. You can substitute 2 cups (500 mL) canned or frozen corn for fresh, adding it just before serving.

2-1/2 lb	chicken thighs	1.25 kg	1	can (19 oz/540 mL) chick-peas, drained and rinsed	1
4 tsp	vegetable oil	20 mL	1	can (19 oz/540 mL) red kidney beans, drained and rinsed	1
4	carrots, thickly sliced	4			
2	onions, chopped	2	3	stalks celery, sliced	3
2	cloves garlic, minced	2	1	sweet green pepper, chopped	1
4 tsp	chili powder	20 mL			
1-1/2 tsp	ground cumin	7 mL	3 tbsp	chopped fresh coriander	50 mL
1/2 tsp	dried oregano	2 mL			
1/4 tsp	(approx) salt	1 mL			
Pinch	(approx) pepper	Pinch			
1	can (28 oz/796 mL) tomatoes	1			
3 tbsp	tomato paste	50 mL			
2 tbsp	lime juice	25 mL			
2	cobs corn, cut into 1-1/2-inch (4 cm) lengths	2			
1 tsp	granulated sugar	5 mL			

● Skin and bone chicken; cut into large bite-size pieces. In Dutch oven, heat 1 tbsp (15 mL) of the oil over medium-high heat; brown chicken, in batches, for 5 minutes. Remove and set aside.

● Add remaining oil to pot; cook carrots, onions and garlic over medium heat, stirring occasionally, for 3 minutes or until onions are softened. Add chili powder, cumin, oregano, salt and pepper; cook, stirring, for 1 minute.

● Add tomatoes, crushing with fork; add tomato paste, lime juice, corn, sugar and chicken. Bring to boil, scraping up brown bits from bottom of pan. Reduce heat to low; cover and simmer for 20 minutes.

● Add chick-peas, kidney beans, celery, green pepper and 2 tbsp (25 mL) of the coriander; cover and simmer, stirring occasionally, for 30 minutes or until vegetables are tender. Season with salt and pepper to taste. Garnish with remaining coriander. Makes 8 servings.

COOK-YOUR-OWN BEANS

● Beans, including chick-peas, are handy in cans, and the 19-ounce (540 mL) ones hold about 2 cups (500 mL) drained. You can also cook your own, at a fraction of the cost.

● Simply rinse and soak dried beans overnight in three times their volume of cold water. Or, for a quick soak, bring to boil and boil gently for 2 minutes. Remove from heat, cover and let stand for 1 hour.

● Once beans have soaked for required time, drain off water. In saucepan, cover beans again with three times their new volume of water and bring to boil. Reduce heat and simmer, covered, for 1 to 2 hours depending on the variety or until beans are tender.

● Drained cooked beans can be frozen in handy 1-cup (250 mL) amounts for adding to soups, stews, pastas and burritos.

● To calculate yields, keep in mind that 1 cup (250 mL) dried beans simmers into 2 cups (500 mL) cooked beans.

Chicken Meatball Stew ▼

Chock-full of vegetables and beans, this heart-healthy family dish is ready in less than an hour. If black beans are unavailable, use a 19-ounce (540 mL) can of kidney beans.

1 tbsp	olive oil	15 mL
2	onions, cut into wedges	2
4	cloves garlic, minced	4
2 cups	cubed peeled squash	500 mL
1-1/2 cups	chicken stock	375 mL
1/2 cup	parboiled rice	125 mL
1/2 tsp	dried basil	2 mL
1/4 tsp	each dried marjoram, salt and pepper	1 mL
Pinch	hot pepper flakes	Pinch
1	can (28 oz/796 mL) stewed tomatoes	1
1	can (15 oz/425 mL) black beans, drained and rinsed	1
3 tbsp	tomato paste	50 mL
2	zucchini, sliced	2

CHICKEN MEATBALLS		
1	egg	1
1 lb	ground chicken	500 g
1/4 cup	dry bread crumbs	50 mL
1 tbsp	chopped fresh parsley	15 mL
1 tsp	salt	5 mL
1/4 tsp	each dried basil and pepper	1 mL

● In large saucepan or Dutch oven, heat oil over medium heat; cook onions and garlic, stirring, for 3 minutes or until just starting to soften.

● Stir in squash, chicken stock, rice, basil, marjoram, salt, pepper and hot pepper flakes; bring to boil. Reduce heat, cover and simmer for 20 minutes or until rice is almost tender.

● CHICKEN MEATBALLS: Meanwhile, in large bowl, beat egg; mix in chicken, bread crumbs, parsley, salt, basil and pepper. With damp hands, shape into 1-inch (2.5 cm) balls; arrange on lightly greased baking sheet. Bake in 350°F (180°C) oven, turning once, for 15 minutes.

● Stir tomatoes, black beans, tomato paste, zucchini and meatballs into rice mixture. Cover and cook over medium-low heat, stirring occasionally, for 20 to 25 minutes or until zucchini is tender. Makes 6 servings.

Easy Chicken and Rice ▲

1 tbsp	vegetable oil	15 mL
2	chicken legs	2
	Salt and pepper	
2/3 cup	long grain rice	150 mL
1	onion, chopped	1
1	clove garlic, minced	1
1/4 tsp	each dried oregano and thyme	1 mL
1	can (19 oz/540 mL) kidney beans, drained and rinsed	1
1	can (10 oz/284 mL) mushrooms, drained	1
1-1/3 cups	water	325 mL
	Paprika	

● In skillet, heat oil over medium-high heat; add chicken and brown all over, about 10 minutes. Season with salt and pepper to taste. Remove from skillet; set aside.

● Pour off all but 1 tbsp (15 mL) fat from skillet. Add rice, onion, garlic, oregano and thyme; cook, stirring, over medium heat for about 3 minutes or until rice is browned. Stir in kidney beans, mushrooms and water.

● Nestle chicken in rice mixture; sprinkle with paprika to taste. Bring to boil; cover, reduce heat to low and simmer for 30 to 40 minutes or until juices run clear when chicken is pierced. Makes 2 servings.

Everything in one pot is ideal for the busy cook, whether the dish is for two or eight. While the chicken and rice simmer, toss a quick spinach salad to enjoy as an appetizer.

Chicken Pot Pie ▶

This lightened-up version is still filled with all the satisfying ingredients and flavors that spell comfort in a chicken pot pie.

6 cups	chicken stock	1.5 L
3 lb	chicken thighs and breasts	1.5 kg
4	red potatoes, cut into 1-inch (2.5 cm) cubes	4
2 cups	chopped carrots	500 mL
4	stalks celery, thickly sliced	4
2 cups	halved mushrooms	500 mL
6	green onions, chopped	6
1	sweet red pepper, cut into chunks	1
1/4 cup	butter or vegetable oil	50 mL
3/4 cup	all-purpose flour	175 mL
2 cups	frozen peas	500 mL
2 cups	frozen corn niblets	500 mL
1/2 cup	chopped fresh parsley	125 mL
1 tsp	dried thyme	5 mL
1/2 tsp	dried savory	2 mL
	Salt and pepper	

BISCUIT CRUST		
1 cup	all-purpose flour	250 mL
1/2 cup	whole wheat flour	125 mL
1 tbsp	baking powder	15 mL
1-1/2 tsp	crumbled dried rosemary	7 mL
3/4 tsp	pepper	4 mL
1/2 tsp	baking soda	2 mL
1/2 tsp	salt	2 mL
1/4 cup	cold butter	50 mL
4	green onions, chopped	4
3/4 cup	buttermilk	175 mL
1	egg white	1
	Sesame seeds	

● BISCUIT CRUST: In large bowl, combine all-purpose and whole wheat flours, baking powder, rosemary, pepper, baking soda and salt. Using pastry blender, cut in butter until mixture resembles coarse crumbs. Stir in onions. With fork, stir in buttermilk until soft, slightly sticky dough forms. Knead on floured surface 10 times until smooth.

● Place waxed paper on baking sheet. Trace outline of 12-cup (3 L) oval baking dish or 13- x 9-inch (3 L) glass baking dish on paper; flour paper. Press dough onto paper to fit just inside line; cut diagonal lines right through dough to form diamond shapes. Cover dough and refrigerate while preparing filling.

● In stockpot, bring stock to boil. Add chicken thighs and reduce heat to medium-low; cover and simmer for 10 minutes. Add breasts and simmer for 25 minutes or until no longer pink inside; remove chicken and let cool.

● In stock, simmer potatoes, carrots and celery for 20 to 25 minutes or until tender-crisp. Add mushrooms, green onions and red pepper; simmer for 2 minutes. Drain in colander, reserving liquid. Skim off fat from liquid. Discard skin from chicken. Remove meat; cut into bite-size chunks.

● In same pot, melt butter over medium heat. Sprinkle with flour; cook, stirring, for 2 minutes. Add 5 cups (1.25 L) reserved liquid, 1/2 cup (125 mL) at a time, whisking until smooth; cook, whisking, for 5 to 8 minutes or until sauce has thickened.

● Combine potato mixture, sauce, peas, corn, parsley, thyme, savory, and salt and pepper to taste. Spoon into baking dish. Invert chilled dough onto stew; peel off paper.

● Brush with egg white; sprinkle with sesame seeds. Bake on baking sheet in 450°F (230°C) oven for 20 minutes or until bubbly and crust is golden. Makes 8 servings.

Microwave Chicken and Rotini

1-3/4 lb	chicken thighs	875 g
1	onion, chopped	1
1 tsp	vegetable oil	5 mL
1	can (19 oz/540 mL) stewed tomatoes	1
1 cup	water	250 mL
1-1/4 tsp	dried basil	6 mL
2 cups	rotini pasta	500 mL
1-1/2 cups	shredded spinach	375 mL
2 tbsp	freshly grated Parmesan cheese	25 mL
1/2 tsp	salt	2 mL
1/4 tsp	pepper	1 mL

● Skin and bone chicken; cut into bite-size pieces.

● In 12-cup (3 L) microwaveable casserole, combine chicken, onion and oil; cover and microwave at High, stirring once, for 6 to 8 minutes or until juices run clear when chicken is pierced. Transfer to bowl.

● Add tomatoes, water and basil to casserole; cover and microwave at High for 6 to 8 minutes or until boiling. Stir in pasta; cover and microwave at High for 9 to 11 minutes or until tender but firm.

● Return chicken mixture to casserole; microwave at High for 30 seconds. Stir in spinach, cheese, salt and pepper; cover and let stand for 5 minutes. Makes 4 servings.

Dress up this quick-to-make supper with an extra sprinkle of cheese, and serve with a green salad and toasted bagels. If you're short of time, purchase inexpensive boneless thighs.

Oriental Fondue ▶

This everyone-cooks meal is one of the easiest and most fun to eat. By the time the vegetables and chicken are ready, the broth has absorbed rich flavors and becomes a delicious soup. Serve with bowls of hot long grain rice.

6	boneless skinless chicken breasts	6
4	carrots	4
2	small zucchini	2
3 cups	broccoli florets	750 mL
2 cups	mushrooms	500 mL
8 cups	chicken stock	2 L
	Peanut Sauce (recipe follows)	
2-1/2 cups	fine egg noodles	625 mL
1 tbsp	light soy sauce	15 mL
1 tsp	sesame oil	5 mL
	Salt and pepper	

● Cut chicken across the grain into very thin slices; place on platter.

● Using vegetable peeler, peel carrots and zucchini lengthwise into ribbons; arrange on separate platter with broccoli and mushrooms.

● In fondue pot, electric wok or skillet in center of table, bring stock to boil. Using fondue forks or chopsticks, let each person cook a few pieces of chicken and vegetables at a time for 1 to 2 minutes or until chicken is no longer pink inside and vegetables are tender-crisp. Serve with Peanut Sauce.

● When chicken is eaten, add any remaining vegetables and noodles to stock; cook for 4 to 6 minutes or until tender but firm. Stir in soy sauce, sesame oil, and salt and pepper to taste. Serve in heated soup bowls. Makes 6 servings.

PEANUT SAUCE		
1/4 cup	peanut butter	50 mL
2 tbsp	each rice vinegar, liquid honey and soy sauce	25 mL
2 tbsp	chicken stock or water	25 mL
1 tbsp	minced gingerroot	15 mL
1 tsp	sesame oil	5 mL
1	clove garlic, minced	1

● Whisk together peanut butter, vinegar, honey, soy sauce, chicken stock, ginger, sesame oil and garlic. Makes 3/4 cup (175 mL).

TIP: Be sure to keep raw chicken on separate plates and away from other food.

ORIENTAL INGREDIENTS

Sesame Oil
● When buying sesame oil to use in Oriental dishes, look for the dark oil with a distinct roasted sesame seed flavor.
● Oriental groceries and many supermarkets carry this oil on their shelves. Store opened bottles in refrigerator.

Soy Sauce
● Which soy sauce to use? In most stir-fries, light soy sauce is called for. This is not sodium-reduced soy sauce, although it can be used if desired. Rather, it is lighter in color than the dark soy sauce used in barbecue sauces and glazes.
● To tell the difference, turn the bottle sideways and then back upright. If the film of liquid on the neck of the bottle clears almost immediately, it's light soy sauce. If it forms a dark film on the glass that is slow in clearing, the soy sauce is the dark, heavy variety.
● If the kind of soy sauce is not specified, use light.

Chicken Niçoise ▼

This one-pot dish celebrates the flavors of the south of France — garlic, tomatoes, bay leaves, onions and olives. Serve with crusty bread to absorb the memorable sauce.

8	chicken thighs	8	2 cups	quartered mushrooms	500 mL
1/3 cup	lemon juice	75 mL	1	can (19 oz/540 mL) tomatoes, drained and chopped	1
2	cloves garlic, minced	2			
1/2 tsp	each dried basil and thyme	2 mL	1	can (14 oz/398 mL) large pitted black olives, drained and halved	1
1	bay leaf	1			
4 tsp	olive oil	20 mL	1-1/2 cups	frozen cut green beans	375 mL
4	small onions, quartered	4		Salt and pepper	

● Remove skin from chicken; place in shallow glass dish. Sprinkle with lemon juice, garlic, basil and thyme; add bay leaf. Let stand for 10 minutes. Remove chicken from marinade, reserving marinade.

● In large deep skillet or Dutch oven, heat oil over medium-high heat; cook chicken, turning once, for 5 to 7 minutes or until golden brown. Remove chicken and set aside.

● Add onions and mushrooms to skillet; cook, stirring, for 2 minutes. Add marinade and tomatoes, stirring to scrape up brown bits from bottom of pan. Return chicken to pan along with olives; bring to boil. Reduce heat, cover and simmer for 40 minutes.

● Increase heat to medium-low; add green beans, pushing down into liquid. Cook, uncovered, for 5 minutes or until beans are tender-crisp. Skim off any fat; discard bay leaf. Season with salt and pepper to taste. Makes 6 servings.

Hungarian Chicken Skillet Stew

4	chicken legs	4
4	slices bacon, diced	4
2	stalks celery, chopped	2
2	carrots, thinly sliced	2
1	onion, chopped	1
1	sweet green pepper, chopped	1
1 tbsp	each paprika and tomato paste	15 mL
1 cup	chicken stock	250 mL
1/2 cup	sour cream	125 mL
2 tbsp	all-purpose flour	25 mL
	Salt and pepper	
2 tbsp	chopped fresh parsley	25 mL

● Separate chicken legs at joint. In large skillet, cook bacon over medium-high heat for 2 to 4 minutes or until crisp; remove and set aside. Add chicken to skillet; cook, turning often, for about 7 minutes or until browned on all sides. Add to bacon.

● Drain off all but 1 tsp (5 mL) fat from skillet. Cook celery, carrots, onion and green pepper for 3 minutes or until softened. Stir in paprika and tomato paste; stir in stock and bring to boil.

● Return chicken and bacon to skillet; reduce heat to low, cover and simmer for 1 hour or until juices run clear when chicken is pierced. Remove chicken to warmed platter; cover to keep warm. Skim off any fat from pan juices.

● Whisk sour cream with flour until smooth; whisk into pan juices and cook over low heat, stirring, for about 2 minutes or until thickened. Season with salt and pepper to taste. Pour over chicken; garnish with parsley. Makes 4 servings.

Egg noodles speckled with parsley or poppy seeds do exactly what starchy side dishes ought to do with stew — add to the flavor and enjoyment of the dish by providing the tasty sauce with something to cling to!

Herbed Chicken Stew

4	slices bacon, diced	4
3 lb	chicken pieces	1.5 kg
2	large onions, chopped	2
2	cloves garlic, minced	2
1/4 cup	dry white vermouth or chicken stock	50 mL
1	can (19 oz/540 mL) tomatoes	1
1 tsp	each crumbled dried rosemary and sage	5 mL
1/4 tsp	each salt and pepper	1 mL
2	zucchini, diced	2
1/4 cup	minced fresh parsley	50 mL
1/3 cup	freshly grated Parmesan cheese	75 mL

● In Dutch oven, cook bacon over medium-high heat for 2 to 4 minutes or until crisp; remove and set aside. Add chicken to pan; cook, turning often, for about 7 minutes or until browned on all sides. Add to bacon.

● Pour off any fat from pan. Cook onions and garlic over medium heat for 4 minutes or until softened. Return bacon and chicken to pan; add vermouth and tomatoes, breaking up with spoon. Add rosemary, sage, salt and pepper; bring to boil, stirring to scrape up brown bits.

● Reduce heat and simmer, stirring occasionally, for about 30 minutes or until juices run clear when chicken is pierced. With slotted spoon, transfer chicken to serving dish and keep warm.

● Add zucchini and bring to boil; cook for about 5 minutes or until sauce is slightly thickened. Spoon over chicken; sprinkle with parsley. Pass cheese separately. Makes 6 servings.

This quick tomatoey stew is delicious over polenta (see below). Use either a whole cut-up chicken (it's cheaper), or buy parts, preferably legs or thighs for their great flavor.

QUICK POLENTA

Bring 3 cups (750 mL) chicken stock or water to boil; gradually whisk in 1 cup (250 mL) yellow cornmeal. Reduce heat to medium and simmer, stirring constantly, for about 10 minutes or until thickened and smooth. Season with salt and pepper to taste. Makes 4 to 6 servings.

Chicken and Sausage Jambalaya

Jambalaya is a great dish for entertaining buffet-style. It's easy to eat, and just needs a green salad and crusty baguette to keep everyone content. Up the spiciness when it's adults only.

TIP: Spicy sausage adds so much to a rice-and-chicken dish like jambalaya. Chorizo, spicy Italian and Hungarian sausages are the best picks.

2 tbsp	vegetable oil	25 mL
8	chicken thighs	8
3/4 lb	spicy sausage, cut into 1-inch (2.5 cm) pieces	375 g
1	onion, chopped	1
2	cloves garlic, minced	2
1	sweet green pepper, chopped	1
2	each carrots and celery, chopped	2
1 tsp	dried thyme	5 mL
1/2 tsp	each salt and dried oregano	2 mL
1/4 tsp	each hot pepper flakes and pepper	1 mL
1	can (19 oz/540 mL) tomatoes	1
1 cup	chicken stock	250 mL
2 tbsp	tomato paste	25 mL
1 cup	parboiled rice	250 mL
2 tbsp	chopped fresh parsley	25 mL

● In large skillet, heat oil over medium-high heat; brown chicken all over. Remove to plate.

● Add sausages to skillet; cook, stirring occasionally, for 5 to 7 minutes or until browned and no longer pink inside. Add to chicken.

● Drain off all but 1 tbsp (15 mL) fat from skillet; cook onion, garlic, green pepper, carrots, celery, thyme, salt, oregano, hot pepper flakes and pepper, stirring, for 3 to 5 minutes or until softened. Stir in tomatoes, breaking up with spoon. Stir in chicken stock and tomato paste; bring to boil.

● Return chicken and sausage to skillet; add rice. Reduce heat to low; cook, covered, for 45 to 60 minutes or until rice is tender and juices run clear when chicken is pierced. Sprinkle with parsley. Makes 6 servings.

Tropical Chicken and Apple Curry ▶

Serve this mild curry over rice with a selection of toppings — toasted coconut, mango, chutney, raisins, sliced bananas, toasted slivered almonds, and yogurt with cucumber and mint.

6	chicken legs	6
1/4 cup	all-purpose flour	50 mL
1 tsp	salt	5 mL
1/2 tsp	pepper	2 mL
2 tbsp	vegetable oil	25 mL
3	cloves garlic, minced	3
1 tbsp	chopped gingerroot	15 mL
2	onions, chopped	2
2 tbsp	curry powder	25 mL
1/2 tsp	cinnamon	2 mL
1/4 tsp	ground cumin	1 mL
1	can (10 oz/284 mL) stewed tomatoes	1
1	can (14 oz/398 mL) coconut milk	1
3	apples, cored and chopped	3
1 tbsp	packed brown sugar	15 mL
1/4 cup	chopped fresh coriander or parsley	50 mL

● Remove skin from chicken; separate legs at joint. In paper bag, combine flour, salt and pepper; shake chicken in mixture to coat.

● In large skillet, heat 1 tbsp (15 mL) of the oil over medium-high heat; cook chicken for 10 minutes or until browned all over. Remove and set aside.

● Add remaining oil, garlic, ginger and onions to skillet; cook over medium heat, stirring, for 3 minutes or until onions are softened. Stir in curry powder, cinnamon and cumin; cook for 1 minute. Add tomatoes and coconut milk, stirring to scrape up brown bits; bring to boil.

● Return chicken to pan; cover and cook over low heat, turning once, for 15 to 20 minutes or until juices run clear when chicken is pierced. Add apples and sugar. Bring to boil over medium-high heat; cook for 5 minutes or until apples are tender. Stir in coriander. Makes 6 servings.

Great Grills

With its crisp golden skin, great smoky flavor and ease of preparation out-of-doors, barbecued chicken has become a beloved summer classic.

Sweet and Sour Glazed Chicken

Starting chicken in the microwave and finishing it on the barbecue is one sure way of keeping chicken juicy and moist inside, yet crisp and golden brown on the outside.

4	chicken quarters (2 lb/1 kg total)	4
1/2 cup	finely chopped onion	125 mL
2 tsp	vegetable oil	10 ml
2 tbsp	packed brown sugar	25 mL
2 tbsp	tomato paste	25 mL
2 tbsp	white wine vinegar	25 mL
2 tsp	dry mustard	10 mL
1 cup	chili sauce	250 mL

● Remove wing tips, reserving for another use. In shallow microwaveable dish, arrange chicken with thickest parts at edge; cover and microwave at Medium-High (70%) for 12 minutes, turning and rearranging once.

Let stand for 5 minutes. If necessary, microwave for 1 to 3 minutes longer or until juices run clear when chicken is pierced. Remove skin.

● Meanwhile, in 4-cup (1 L) measure, microwave onion in oil at High for 2 minutes. Blend in sugar, tomato paste, vinegar and mustard; stir in chili sauce. Microwave at High for 3 to 4 minutes or until boiling; brush some over chicken.

● Place chicken on greased grill over medium heat; cover and cook, turning and basting with sauce, for 6 to 8 minutes or until browned. Serve with remaining sauce. Makes 4 servings.

Hazelnut-Stuffed Chicken Halves

A crunchy under-the-skin stuffing flavors the chicken as it cooks. Serve this special-occasion bird with asparagus or sugar snap peas and grilled new potatoes.

1/2 cup	hazelnuts	125 mL
3 tbsp	butter	50 mL
1 cup	chopped mushrooms	250 mL
2	green onions, chopped	2
1/2 cup	dry bread crumbs	125 mL
1 tbsp	chopped fresh thyme	15 mL
	Salt and pepper	
1	chicken, halved (about 3 lb/1.5 kg)	1
1 tbsp	vegetable oil	15 mL

● Spread hazelnuts on baking sheet; bake in 350°F (180°C) oven for 10 minutes. Place in terry cloth towel and rub off most of the skins. Chop nuts finely; set aside.

● In skillet, melt butter over medium heat; cook mushrooms and green onions for 3 minutes or until softened. Stir in hazelnuts, bread crumbs, thyme, and salt and pepper to taste.

● Starting at breast end of chicken, gently loosen skin over breast, thigh and as far up drumstick as possible, keeping skin attached to breastbone as much as possible. Pack stuffing under loosened skin.

● Brush chicken lightly with oil. Place, skin side down, on greased grill over medium heat; cover and cook for 20 minutes. Turn and cook for 20 to 30 minutes longer or until meat thermometer inserted in thigh registers 185°F (85°C). Makes 4 servings.

Perfect Barbecued Chicken ▲

1	chicken (4 to 5 lb/2 to 2.2 kg)	1
1/4 cup	white wine, vermouth or chicken stock	50 mL
1/4 cup	white wine vinegar	50 mL
1/4 cup	vegetable oil	50 mL
1	onion, chopped	1
2 tsp	chopped fresh rosemary	10 mL

● Remove neck and giblets from chicken; pat chicken dry inside and out.

● Stir together wine, vinegar, oil, onion and rosemary; brush some of the mixture inside cavity. Tie legs together with string; tuck wings under back.

● Using Indirect Cooking Method (sidebar, this page), place chicken, breast side down, on greased grill over medium heat. Brush with some of the wine mixture; cover and cook for 20 minutes.

● Turn chicken and baste. Cover and cook, basting frequently, for 1 to 1-1/4 hours or until meat thermometer inserted in thickest part of thigh registers 185°F (85°C). Remove from heat and place on cutting board; tent with foil and let stand for 10 minutes before carving. Makes 6 servings.

*P*erfect says it all — *succulent chicken with a coppery burnished skin. The secret is the Indirect Cooking Method (sidebar, this page), which allows the chicken to cook through before the outside is charred.*

INDIRECT COOKING METHOD

● **For gas barbecues with two or more burners**: On one side of barbecue, place food on grill over drip pan; turn off burner under drip pan, leaving other burner(s) on. Cook as directed.

● **For charcoal barbecues with covers**: Move hot coals to sides of barbecue; put drip pan between coals. Place food on grill over drip pan. Cook as directed.

Jerk Chicken Legs

6	chicken legs	6
1 tbsp	ground allspice	15 mL
1 tbsp	hot pepper flakes	15 mL
1 tbsp	granulated sugar	15 mL
1 tsp	salt	5 mL
1/2 tsp	each nutmeg and cinnamon	2 mL
2	cloves garlic, minced	2
3/4 cup	vinegar	175 mL
1/2 cup	orange juice	125 mL
1/4 cup	each vegetable oil, soy sauce and lemon juice	50 mL
1	onion, finely chopped	1
4	green onions, finely chopped	4

● Separate chicken legs at joint. In large bowl, combine allspice, hot pepper flakes, sugar, salt, nutmeg, cinnamon and garlic; whisk in vinegar, orange juice, oil, soy sauce, lemon juice, onion and green onions.

● Add chicken, turning to coat. Cover and marinate in refrigerator for at least 8 hours or up to 24 hours, turning occasionally. Let stand at room temperature for 30 minutes.

● Reserving marinade in small saucepan, place chicken on greased grill over medium heat; cook, turning often, for 25 to 30 minutes or until juices run clear when chicken is pierced.

● Meanwhile, bring reserved marinade to boil; boil for 1 minute. Serve as sauce with chicken. Makes 6 servings.

Jamaican in origin, this dish can be prepared using any chicken parts or even pork. To go for the burn, up the hot pepper flakes.

Jump-Up Chicken Legs ◄

4	chicken legs	4
1 cup	ketchup	250 mL
1/2 cup	pineapple juice	125 mL
1/2 cup	water	125 mL
3 tbsp	Dijon mustard	50 mL
1 tbsp	chopped gingerroot	15 mL
4	cloves garlic, minced	4
1	onion, minced	1
1	sweet red or green pepper, minced	1
1/2 tsp	salt	2 mL
1/4 tsp	pepper	1 mL
1/4 tsp	hot pepper flakes	1 mL

● Remove skin from chicken. Arrange legs in single layer in greased baking dish. Bake in 375°F (190°C) oven for 30 to 40 minutes or until juices run clear when chicken is pierced. *(Chicken can be prepared to this point, refrigerated immediately and stored for up to 1 day.)*

● In skillet, combine ketchup, pineapple juice, water, mustard, ginger, garlic, onion, red pepper, salt, pepper and hot pepper flakes; bring to boil. Reduce heat to medium; cook for 5 to 8 minutes or until thickened. *(Sauce can be cooled, covered and refrigerated for up to 2 days.)* Reserve 1 cup (250 mL) to serve with chicken.

● Place chicken on greased grill over medium heat; cook for 2 minutes on each side. Brush generously with some of the remaining sauce; turn and cook for 5 minutes. Brush with sauce; turn and cook for 5 minutes longer. Serve with reserved sauce. Makes 4 servings.

St. Lucia in the Caribbean is famous for its Friday night jump-ups — street parties which feature sizzling grilled chicken crisped in a fabulous ginger, pineapple and mustard sauce.

TIMESAVING TWO-STEP COOKING

Cook chicken through in either the microwave or the oven. Then, according to your schedule, immediately barbecue until crisped on the outside, or refrigerate immediately and store for up to 1 day. Let stand at room temperature for 30 minutes before brushing with sauce and crisping on the grill.

Teriyaki Ginger Chicken

To balance the Oriental flavors, serve the chicken with rice and a refreshing salad of greens, orange slices, thinly sliced onion rings and toasted almonds.

3 tbsp	teriyaki sauce	50 mL
1	egg white, lightly beaten	1
1 tbsp	cornstarch	15 mL
2 tsp	minced gingerroot	10 mL
1	clove garlic, minced	1
4	chicken legs	4

● In shallow dish, stir together teriyaki sauce, egg white, cornstarch, ginger and garlic; add chicken, turning to coat. Cover and marinate in refrigerator for at least 1 hour or up to 8 hours, turning occasionally. Let stand at room temperature for 30 minutes.

● Reserving marinade, place chicken, meaty side down, on greased grill over medium heat; cover and cook for 10 minutes.

● Turn and brush with marinade. Cover and cook, brushing occasionally with marinade, for 15 to 20 minutes or until juices run clear when chicken is pierced. Makes 4 servings.

Grilled Piri Piri Chicken

Don't be afraid of the amount of garlic — it mellows and sweetens up as it cooks.

3 tbsp	grated lemon rind	45 mL
1/4 cup	lemon juice	50 mL
1	head garlic (about 14 cloves), minced	1
2 tbsp	olive oil	25 mL
1 tbsp	hot pepper flakes	15 mL
1 tsp	salt	5 mL
6	chicken legs or breasts	6

● In small bowl, combine lemon rind and juice, garlic, olive oil, hot pepper flakes and salt. Rub over chicken, pushing some of the mixture under skin. Place in shallow dish; cover and marinate in refrigerator for at least 8 hours or up to 24 hours. Let stand at room temperature for 30 minutes.

● Place chicken on greased grill over medium heat; cover and cook for about 15 minutes on each side or until juices run clear when legs are pierced or until breasts are no longer pink inside. Makes 6 servings.

Tangy Peppercorn Chicken ▶

You may think there's too much of everything in this marinade — but cooking tames the tang of the vinegar and blends the robust flavors of the mustard, peppercorns and garlic.

8	chicken legs	8
3/4 cup	balsamic vinegar or red wine vinegar	175 mL
3 tbsp	olive oil	50 mL
2 tbsp	Dijon mustard	25 mL
6	cloves garlic, minced	6
1 tbsp	coarsely cracked black peppercorns	15 mL
2 tsp	each dried thyme and oregano	10 mL
1/2 tsp	salt	2 mL

● Place chicken in large shallow dish. Whisk together vinegar, oil, mustard, garlic, peppercorns, thyme, oregano and salt; pour over chicken. Cover and marinate in refrigerator for at least 2 hours or up to 8 hours, turning occasionally. Let stand at room temperature for 30 minutes.

● Reserving marinade, place chicken on greased grill over medium heat; cook, basting occasionally with marinade, for about 20 minutes on each side or until juices run clear when chicken is pierced. Makes 8 servings.

Orange Cumin Chicken

A citrus-based marinade enhances the flavor of grilled chicken. Serve with a pasta salad and green beans.

6	chicken legs, skinned	6
2 tsp	grated orange rind	10 mL
1 tsp	grated lime rind	5 mL
1/2 cup	orange juice	125 mL
2 tbsp	lime juice	25 mL
2 tbsp	liquid honey	25 mL
2 tbsp	tomato paste	25 mL
2 tsp	ground cumin	10 mL
3	cloves garlic, minced	3
1 tsp	salt	5 mL
1/2 tsp	pepper	2 mL
1/4 cup	chopped fresh coriander or parsley	50 mL

● Place chicken in shallow dish. Combine orange and lime rinds and juices, honey, tomato paste, cumin, garlic, salt and pepper; pour over chicken, turning to coat. Cover and marinate in refrigerator for at least 4 hours or up to 24 hours, turning occasionally. Let stand at room temperature for 30 minutes.

● Reserving marinade, sprinkle coriander over chicken. Place chicken on greased grill over medium heat; cover and cook, turning halfway through and basting once with marinade, for about 30 minutes or until juices run clear when chicken is pierced. Makes 6 servings.

Citrus Mustard Chicken

Use this marinade on chicken legs or halves, too. Simply grill legs until juices run clear when pierced. Chicken halves are done when meat thermometer inserted in thickest part of thigh registers 185°F (85°C).

1/4 cup	lemon juice	50 mL
1/4 cup	Dijon mustard	50 mL
3 tbsp	olive oil	45 mL
4	chicken breasts	4
1/4 cup	marmalade	50 mL

● In shallow dish, mix together lemon juice, mustard and oil; add chicken, turning to coat. Cover and marinate in refrigerator for at least 2 hours or up to 8 hours, turning occasionally. Let stand at room temperature for 30 minutes.

● Place chicken, skin side down, on greased grill over medium heat; cover and cook, turning once, for 20 minutes. Brush with marmalade; cook for 5 to 10 minutes or until no longer pink inside. Makes 4 servings.

Piña Colada Kabobs

Pineapple and coconut flatter the flavor of grilled chicken. For color, add chunks of sweet red or green pepper to each skewer.

4	boneless skinless chicken breasts	4
1 cup	unsweetened coconut milk or yogurt	250 mL
2 tbsp	chopped fresh mint	25 mL
1 tbsp	lime juice	15 mL
1/2 tsp	cracked peppercorns	2 mL
6	small onions, blanched and halved	6
1	fresh pineapple	1

● Cut each chicken breast into 4 large chunks. In bowl, mix coconut milk, mint, lime juice and peppercorns; add chicken, turning to coat. Cover and marinate in refrigerator for at least 2 hours or up to 8 hours, stirring occasionally. Let stand at room temperature for 30 minutes.

● Peel pineapple and cut into 2-inch (5 cm) chunks. Reserving marinade, alternately thread chicken, onions and pineapple onto 4 metal skewers. Place skewers on greased grill over medium heat; cover and cook for 10 minutes. Turn and brush with marinade; cook for 7 to 12 minutes longer or until chicken is no longer pink inside. Makes 4 servings.

Really Hot Grilled Wings

1 cup	ketchup	250 mL
1/2 cup	water	125 mL
1	onion, finely chopped	1
1	clove garlic, minced	1
2 tbsp	packed brown sugar	25 mL
2 tbsp	vinegar	25 mL
2 tbsp	lemon juice	25 mL
1 tbsp	Worcestershire sauce	15 mL
1 tsp	dry mustard	5 mL
1 tsp	cayenne pepper	5 mL
1 tsp	chili powder	5 mL
2-1/2 lb	chicken wings	1.25 kg

● In saucepan, bring ketchup, water, onion, garlic, sugar, vinegar, lemon juice, Worcestershire sauce, mustard, cayenne and chili powder to boil, stirring often. Reduce heat to medium-low; simmer for 10 minutes. Set aside 3/4 cup (175 mL) for dipping.

● Meanwhile, remove tips from wings. Arrange 8 wings on microwaveable roasting rack or large plate; cover and microwave at High for 5 minutes or until no longer pink inside. Repeat with remaining wings. (Alternatively, cover wings with cold water; bring to boil and simmer for 20 minutes.)

● Place chicken wings on greased grill over medium heat; brush lightly with sauce. Cook, turning and basting often, for 10 minutes or until glazed and crisp. Serve with reserved sauce. Makes 4 servings.

Cayenne pepper governs the hotness of these always-popular wings. Increase or decrease it to please the fans who will be waiting impatiently beside the barbecue.

Pesto Chicken Burgers

1	egg	1
1/2 cup	chopped fresh basil	125 mL
1/4 cup	dry bread crumbs	50 mL
1/4 cup	finely chopped onion	50 mL
1/4 cup	freshly grated Parmesan cheese	50 mL
2 tbsp	water	25 mL
1 tbsp	finely chopped walnuts or pecans	15 mL
2	cloves garlic, minced	2
1/2 tsp	salt	2 mL
1/4 tsp	pepper	1 mL
1 lb	ground chicken	500 g

4	hamburger buns	4
4	slices tomato	4

● In bowl, beat egg; mix in basil, bread crumbs, onion, cheese, water, walnuts, garlic, salt and pepper. Mix in chicken; shape into four 3/4-inch (2 cm) thick patties.

● Place patties on greased grill over medium heat; cook for 6 to 7 minutes per side or until no longer pink inside. Sandwich each patty and tomato slice in bun. Makes 4 servings.

Summer-fresh basil, Parmesan cheese and nuts spell pesto — and pesto spells a great-tasting burger.
See p. 21 for other burgers that are delicious on the grill, too.

CHICKEN ON THE GRILL

● If marinade that flavored raw chicken is then used to brush over chicken as it cooks on the grill, make sure that the chicken cooks for at least 5 minutes after the last application of marinade. This allows the marinade to cook thoroughly.

● If basting brushes used on raw or partially cooked chicken are dipped into sauce or marinade, bring the sauce or marinade to boil and boil for 2 minutes before serving.

● Always use a clean platter to serve cooked chicken. Never serve it on the same plate that held it raw.

Soups and Salads

Nothing highlights chicken's versatility better than soups and salads.
Just add your favorite flavors or experiment with sassy new tastes.

Basic Chicken Stock

Here's one of the easiest ways to make chicken stock — and, unlike cubes, powders and most canned broths, it's made without salt.

2-1/2 lb	chicken necks, backs and wing tips	1.25 kg
8 cups	hot water	2 L
1	each carrot and stalk celery, cut into chunks	1
1	onion, coarsely chopped	1
3	sprigs parsley	3
1	bay leaf	1
1/2 tsp	each dried thyme and whole black peppercorns	2 mL

● In stock pot or large Dutch oven, bring chicken parts, water, carrot, celery, onion, parsley, bay leaf, thyme and peppercorns to simmer; simmer gently, skimming off any foam as it arises, for about 1-1/2 hours. Strain and let cool.

● Cover and refrigerate until fat has congealed on surface. Remove with slotted spoon. *(Stock can be frozen for up to 4 months.)* Makes about 5 cups (1.25 L).

TIP: Save uncooked wing tips, backs, necks and any bones from chickens in an airtight container in the freezer. When you have about 2-1/2 lb (1.25 kg), let them thaw, rinse well and make the stock above.

Poached Chicken and Chicken Stock

It takes a good-size roasting chicken for this recipe. You'll cook up a moist, flavorful bird that's perfect for salads, sandwiches, pot pies and casseroles. And, best of all, you'll have the stock for noodle soup, remedy for whatever ails you. Don't try this with little frying chickens — they haven't been around long enough to flavor the broth.

1	chicken (4-1/2 lb/2.25 kg)	1
14 cups	water	3.5 L
2	carrots, chopped	2
2	stalks celery, chopped	2
1	onion, cut into eighths	1
2	cloves garlic	2
1	piece (1 inch/2.5 cm) gingerroot	1
3	sprigs fresh parsley	3
2	sprigs fresh thyme (or 1/2 tsp/2 mL dried)	2
1	bay leaf	1
1 tsp	salt	5 mL
1/2 tsp	whole black peppercorns	2 mL

● In stock pot or large Dutch oven, cover chicken with water. Bring to boil; skim off froth. Add carrots, celery, onion, garlic, ginger, parsley, thyme, bay leaf, salt and peppercorns. Reduce heat and simmer, partially covered, for 1-1/2 to 2 hours or until juices run clear when chicken thigh is pierced.

● Remove chicken and refrigerate for another use. Strain liquid through cheesecloth-lined sieve into large bowl, pressing vegetables to extract as much liquid as possible. Let cool to room temperature.

● Cover and refrigerate for 8 hours or until fat has congealed on surface. Remove with slotted spoon. *(Stock can be refrigerated for up to 3 days or frozen for up to 3 months.)* Makes 10-1/2 cups (2.6 L).

Quick Chicken Noodle Soup ▼

2 tbsp	butter	25 mL
1/2 cup	chopped onion	125 mL
5 cups	chicken stock	1.25 L
1-1/2 cups	thickly sliced carrots	375 mL
1 cup	sliced celery	250 mL
1 cup	cubed cooked chicken	250 mL
1 cup	egg noodles	250 mL
2	sprigs fresh dill	2
1/2 cup	frozen peas	125 mL
	Salt and pepper	

● In large saucepan, melt butter over medium heat; cook onion for 3 minutes or until softened.

● Add chicken stock; bring to boil. Add carrots, celery and chicken; reduce heat, cover and simmer for 15 minutes or until vegetables are tender.

● Add egg noodles and dill; cook for 6 to 8 minutes or until noodles are tender. Add peas; season with salt and pepper to taste. Makes 4 servings.

C*heers go up from kids everywhere when chicken noodle soup fills their bowls. No wonder. It's fragrant, satisfying, with just enough vegetables to be virtuous — and it makes them feel cosy inside. A perfect remedy for a cold winter's day.*

TIP: Freeze homemade stock in convenient amounts. For stews and soups, freeze in cups and containers. For smaller quantities, freeze in ice cube trays and store in sealed freezer bags.

Chicken and Rice Soup with Lemon

This Greek-inspired chicken and rice soup is thickened with eggs and refreshed with snippets of mint.

1 tbsp	butter	15 mL
1 tbsp	all-purpose flour	15 mL
8 cups	chicken stock	2 L
1/2 cup	long grain rice	125 mL
1/4 cup	lemon juice	50 mL
2	eggs	2
Dash	hot pepper sauce	Dash
1 tbsp	chopped fresh mint or dill	15 mL
	Salt and pepper	

● In large saucepan, melt butter over medium heat; stir in flour and cook, stirring, without browning, for 2 minutes.

● Whisk in stock and bring to boil; stir in rice. Reduce heat and simmer for about 20 minutes or until rice is tender. Add lemon juice.

● In bowl, beat eggs; whisk in about 1 cup (250 mL) of the hot soup. Whisk back into saucepan. Add hot pepper sauce, mint, and salt and pepper to taste. Makes 6 servings.

Main-Course Minestrone

Letting this chunky vegetable, pasta and bean soup sit overnight blends the flavors, but you may need to add up to 1 cup (250 mL) more stock when reheating.

2 tsp	olive oil	10 mL
3 oz	pancetta or bacon, chopped	75 g
1	onion, chopped	1
2	cloves garlic, minced	2
1	each carrot and stalk celery, sliced on diagonal	1
1	bay leaf	1
3/4 tsp	dried basil	4 mL
1/2 tsp	dried oregano	2 mL
1/2 tsp	salt	2 mL
1/4 tsp	pepper	1 mL
4-1/2 cups	chicken stock	1.125 L
1	can (19 oz/540 mL) tomatoes, mashed	1
1	can (19 oz/540 mL) white or red kidney beans, drained and rinsed	1
2	small potatoes, peeled and cubed	2
1 cup	macaroni	250 mL
1	zucchini, cubed	1
1 cup	packed fresh spinach, chopped	250 mL
	Freshly grated Parmesan cheese	

● In large saucepan, heat oil over medium heat; cook pancetta, onion, garlic, carrot and celery for 3 to 5 minutes or until softened. Stir in bay leaf, basil, oregano, salt and pepper; cook, stirring, for 1 minute.

● Add chicken stock and tomatoes; bring to boil. Add kidney beans; reduce heat, cover and simmer for 20 minutes.

● Add potatoes and macaroni; cover and simmer for 10 to 15 minutes or until potatoes are tender.

● Stir in zucchini and spinach; cook for 5 to 7 minutes or until zucchini is tender-crisp. Discard bay leaf. Garnish each bowlful with cheese. Makes 4 servings.

TIP: To make a chunky chicken minestrone, add 1-1/2 cups (375 mL) cubed cooked chicken along with zucchini and spinach.

Thai Chicken Soup

2 tsp	vegetable oil	10 mL
1-1/2 cups	sliced mushrooms	375 mL
1 cup	sliced bok choy	250 mL
1	carrot, thinly sliced on diagonal	1
4	green onions, sliced	4
1 tbsp	minced gingerroot	15 mL
2	cloves garlic, minced	2
Pinch	hot pepper flakes	Pinch
5 cups	chicken stock	1.25 L
1 cup	slivered cooked chicken	250 mL
1 tbsp	soy sauce	15 mL
2 tsp	rice vinegar	10 mL
1/2 tsp	pepper	2 mL
1/4 tsp	sesame oil	1 mL
1/4 tsp	salt	1 mL
1/4 cup	chopped fresh coriander	50 mL
1/4 cup	chopped peanuts	50 mL

● In large saucepan, heat oil over medium heat; cook mushrooms, bok choy, carrot, onions, ginger, garlic and hot pepper flakes for 3 to 5 minutes or until softened.

● Pour in chicken stock; bring to boil. Add chicken; reduce heat and simmer, covered, for 5 to 8 minutes or until vegetables are tender.

● Stir in soy sauce, vinegar, pepper, sesame oil and salt; simmer for 1 minute. Garnish each bowlful with coriander and peanuts. Makes 4 servings.

Chicken soup goes global with a mix of hot, crunchy and refreshing Thai touches.

Chicken Meatball Noodle Soup

1	egg	1
1/4 cup	dry bread crumbs	50 mL
3/4 tsp	salt	4 mL
1/2 tsp	pepper	2 mL
1 lb	ground chicken	500 g
2 tsp	vegetable oil	10 mL
1 cup	chopped leeks or onions	250 mL
2	cloves garlic, minced	2
8 cups	chicken stock	2 L
1-1/2 cups	each sliced carrots and celery	375 mL
3 tbsp	chopped fresh dill	50 mL
1	piece (1 inch/2.5 cm) gingerroot	1
2 cups	egg noodles	500 mL
	Chopped fresh dill	

● In large bowl, beat egg; mix in bread crumbs, salt and pepper. Mix in chicken. With damp hands, form into 1-inch (2.5 cm) balls. Bake on lightly greased baking sheet in 350°F (180°C) oven, turning once, for 15 minutes. Let drain on paper towels.

● Meanwhile, in Dutch oven or large saucepan, heat oil over medium heat; cook leeks and garlic for about 3 minutes or until softened.

● Add stock, carrots, celery, dill and ginger; bring to boil. Reduce heat to medium-low; cover and simmer for 5 minutes.

● Stir in noodles and meatballs; cook for 8 to 10 minutes or until vegetables and noodles are tender. Remove ginger. *(Soup can be cooled and frozen in airtight containers for up to 2 weeks; reheat gently.)* Garnish each serving with chopped dill. Makes 5 to 7 servings.

For supper in a bowl, nothing beats this vegetable-rich, noodle-slurping meatball soup. Ginger and dill add an up-to-date taste.

Curried Chicken Salad

Winter or summer, chicken salad is never out of season. This chunky salad with a curry twist is perfect on a bed of summer greens, or spooned into a lettuce-lined pita to enjoy around a roaring fire.

3 cups	cubed cooked chicken	750 mL
4	stalks celery, sliced	4
2	carrots, grated	2
2 cups	shredded Monterey Jack cheese	500 mL
1 cup	chopped red onion	250 mL
1 cup	raisins	250 mL
1/2 cup	peanuts, chopped	125 mL
	DRESSING	
1/4 cup	mango chutney	50 mL
3/4 cup	light mayonnaise	175 mL
3/4 cup	plain yogurt	175 mL
1 tbsp	curry powder	15 mL
1 tbsp	cider vinegar	15 mL
2 tsp	dry sherry	10 mL

1 tsp	ground coriander	5 mL
1/2 tsp	ground ginger	2 mL
Pinch	each salt and pepper	Pinch

● DRESSING: Press chutney through fine sieve into large bowl to remove any large chunks. Whisk in mayonnaise, yogurt, curry powder, vinegar, sherry, coriander, ginger, salt and pepper.

● Add chicken, celery, carrots, cheese, onion and raisins; toss to coat well. Transfer to serving dish; garnish with nuts. Makes 4 servings.

Barbecued Chicken Salad

Succulent grilled chicken teams up with a summery selection of red, green and yellow peppers, zucchini and red onions.

6	sweet peppers	6
2	zucchini	2
2 tbsp	olive oil	25 mL
1	red onion	1
6	boneless skinless chicken breasts	6
1 tsp	chopped fresh rosemary	5 mL
4 cups	torn romaine lettuce	1 L
	DRESSING	
3 tbsp	balsamic or red wine vinegar	50 mL
1	clove garlic, minced	1
1 tsp	salt	5 mL
1/4 tsp	pepper	1 mL
1/2 cup	olive oil	125 mL

● Place sweet peppers on greased grill over medium-high heat; cook, turning often, for 20 to 25 minutes or until blackened all over. Let cool. Peel, seed and cut into bite-size pieces.

● Meanwhile, cut zucchini in half lengthwise and brush with some of the oil; place on grill and cook for 3 to 4 minutes per side or until tender-crisp.

● Slice onion thickly and brush with some of the oil; place on grill and cook for 3 to 4 minutes per side or until browned.

● Brush chicken with remaining oil and sprinkle with rosemary; place on grill and cook for 6 to 8 minutes per side or until no longer pink inside. Cut zucchini, onion and chicken into bite-size pieces.

● DRESSING: In large bowl, combine vinegar, garlic, salt and pepper; whisk in oil. Add peppers, zucchini, onion and chicken, tossing to coat. *(Salad can be covered and refrigerated for up to 1 day. Let stand at room temperature for 30 minutes before serving.)* Serve on bed of lettuce. Makes 6 servings.

Thai Chicken Salad ▼

1/2 tsp	salt	2 mL
4	skinless chicken breasts	4
4 oz	rice vermicelli	125 g
Half	English cucumber, cut into small strips	Half
1	large sweet red pepper, cut into strips	1
1/4 cup	chopped fresh mint	50 mL
	DRESSING	
1/4 cup	fish sauce	50 mL
3 tbsp	lime juice	45 mL
2 tbsp	packed brown sugar	25 mL
1 tbsp	minced gingerroot	15 mL
1	clove garlic, minced	1
1	jalapeño pepper, seeded and minced	1

● In saucepan, bring 2 cups (500 mL) water and salt to boil; reduce heat to medium-low and poach chicken, turning halfway through, for 13 to 15 minutes or until no longer pink inside. Let cool in broth. Bone chicken; cut into 1-1/2-inch (4 cm) strips.

● In bowl, cover vermicelli with boiling water; let stand for 3 minutes or until softened. Drain well.

● In bowl, combine chicken strips, vermicelli, cucumber, red pepper and mint.

● DRESSING: Combine fish sauce, lime juice, sugar, ginger, garlic and jalapeño pepper; pour over chicken mixture and toss well. Makes 4 servings.

The Thai flavors come from the fish sauce which is as important to this Southeast Asian country as soy sauce is to China. Lime, ginger and hot pepper round out the Thai palate. Garnish this low-fat chicken salad with extra fresh mint and serve on leaf lettuce.

Grilled Chicken Pesto Salad ▼

*N*estle *slices of basil-grilled chicken breast in a rainbow of lettuces for an easy and appealing supper. Garnish with more basil and freshly grated Parmesan cheese.*

4	boneless skinless chicken breasts	4
1/2 cup	fresh basil leaves	125 mL
3 tbsp	red wine vinegar	50 mL
1 tbsp	Dijon mustard	15 mL
2	cloves garlic, minced	2
1/4 tsp	salt	1 mL
Pinch	pepper	Pinch
1/2 cup	olive oil	125 mL
2	sweet potatoes	2
20	cherry tomatoes	20
6 cups	torn lettuce leaves	1.5 L

● Using small knife, cut slit in thickest part of chicken; insert 2 basil leaves into each one. Chop remaining basil; set aside.

● In small bowl, whisk together vinegar, mustard, garlic, salt and pepper; whisk in oil and chopped basil. Brush 2 tbsp (25 mL) of the dressing over chicken; let stand at room temperature for 30 minutes.

● Meanwhile, peel potatoes; cut into 1-1/2-inch (4 cm) cubes. In pot of boiling water, cook potatoes for 8 minutes; drain and refresh under cold water. Thread potatoes and tomatoes onto separate skewers; brush with some of the dressing.

● Place chicken and potato skewers on greased grill over medium-high heat; cook, turning chicken once and potatoes several times, for 10 to 12 minutes or until chicken is no longer pink inside. Remove chicken; let cool.

● Add tomato skewers to grill; cook for 4 minutes, turning once and brushing potatoes and tomatoes with dressing.

● Arrange lettuce on plates. Slice chicken diagonally; fan over lettuce. Add potatoes and tomatoes. Drizzle with remaining dressing. Makes 4 servings.

Oriental Chicken Salad

1/3 cup	soy sauce	75 mL
1/4 cup	tahini	50 mL
2 tbsp	vegetable oil	25 mL
2 tbsp	rice vinegar	25 mL
2 tbsp	dry sherry	25 mL
1 tbsp	sesame oil	15 mL
1 tsp	each ground coriander and ginger	5 mL
2	cloves garlic, minced	2
2 tbsp	(approx) chopped fresh parsley	25 mL
4	cooked boneless skinless chicken breasts, cut into strips	4
1	sweet red pepper, julienned	1
3	carrots, thinly sliced	3
2	stalks celery, thinly sliced	2
4 oz	snow peas, blanched and sliced	125 g
1	bunch green onions, chopped	1
1 cup	water chestnuts, quartered	250 mL
	Lettuce leaves	
1/3 cup	chopped peanuts	75 mL

● In food processor, purée together soy sauce, tahini, vegetable oil, vinegar, sherry, sesame oil, coriander and ginger; stir in garlic and parsley.

● In large serving bowl, combine chicken, red pepper, carrots, celery, snow peas, green onions and water chestnuts; toss gently with dressing.

● Divide among lettuce-lined plates. Sprinkle with more parsley and nuts. Makes 6 to 8 servings.

Tahini, a thick paste made from ground sesame seeds, provides an earthy base for the Oriental grace notes of soy and rice vinegar. Many supermarkets and most health food stores now stock it, as well as Greek and Middle Eastern grocery stores.

Chicken and Black Bean Salad

2	cans (each 15 oz/426 mL) black beans, drained and rinsed	2
3 cups	cubed cooked chicken	750 mL
6	green onions, sliced	6
1	each sweet red and yellow pepper, chopped	1
2	tomatoes, coarsely chopped	2
1/4 cup	chopped fresh coriander	50 mL
	DRESSING	
1	jalapeño pepper, minced	1
1 tsp	grated lime rind	5 mL
1/4 cup	lime juice	50 mL
1	clove garlic, minced	1
1/4 tsp	each salt and pepper	1 mL
1/4 cup	vegetable oil	50 mL

● In large bowl, gently stir together black beans, chicken, onions, red and yellow peppers and tomatoes.

● DRESSING: In small bowl, whisk together jalapeño pepper, lime rind and juice, garlic, salt and pepper; gradually whisk in oil. Pour over salad; add coriander and toss gently. Makes 4 to 6 servings.

Our tastebuds head south and west for a colorful salad with a jalapeño lime dressing.

TIP: It's easiest to open canned black beans and proceed directly with the salad. But if you can't find canned ones, buy the dry beans and cook following the easy directions on p. 24. Soaked black beans require about 1-3/4 hours cooking time.

Snacks and Sandwiches

When the gang arrives, it's chicken time — with crowd-pleasing pâté, lip-smacking wings and sandwiches redesigned for the nineties.

Oriental Lemon Chicken Wings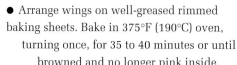

Tangy lemon balances with ginger and hoisin for crispy browned wings. Keep this recipe in mind for potlucks and parties.

4 lb.	chicken wings	2 kg	2	cloves garlic, minced	2
2 tbsp	oyster sauce	25 mL	1 tbsp	sesame seeds (optional)	15 mL
4 tsp	grated gingerroot	20 mL			
1 tbsp	grated lemon rind	15 mL			
1 tbsp	lemon juice	15 mL			
1 tbsp	sesame oil	15 mL			
1 tbsp	hoisin sauce	15 mL			
1 tbsp	soy sauce	15 mL			
1/2 tsp	hot pepper sauce	2 mL			

● Remove tips, excess skin and fat from chicken wings; separate wings at joint.

● In large shallow glass dish, stir together oyster sauce, ginger, lemon rind and juice, sesame oil, hoisin sauce, soy sauce, hot pepper sauce and garlic. Add wings, turning to coat. Cover and marinate in refrigerator for at least 1 hour or up to 8 hours.

● Arrange wings on well-greased rimmed baking sheets. Bake in 375°F (190°C) oven, turning once, for 35 to 40 minutes or until browned and no longer pink inside.

● About 5 minutes before wings are finished, sprinkle with sesame seeds (if using). Makes 6 servings.

Black Bean Chicken Wings

2-1/2 lb	chicken wings	1.25 kg
1/4 cup	Chinese fermented black beans,* drained and rinsed	50 mL
1/3 cup	hoisin sauce	75 mL
1/4 cup	light soy sauce	50 mL
1/4 cup	liquid honey	50 mL
1/4 cup	ketchup	50 mL
2 tbsp	sesame oil	25 mL
2 tbsp	rice vinegar	25 mL
2 tbsp	Dijon mustard	25 mL
2	cloves garlic, minced	2
1/2 tsp	chili oil*	2 mL

● Remove tips, excess skin and fat from chicken wings; separate wings at joint.

● Place beans in bowl just large enough to hold wings; mash with fork. Stir in hoisin sauce, soy sauce, honey, ketchup, sesame oil, vinegar, mustard, garlic and chili oil. Add wings, turning to coat. Cover and marinate in refrigerator for at least 4 hours or up to 24 hours, turning occasionally.

● Reserving marinade, arrange wings on foil-lined rimmed baking sheet. Spoon half of the marinade over wings; bake in 400°F (200°C) oven for 20 minutes.

● Turn wings over and spoon remaining marinade over wings; bake for 20 minutes longer or until browned and no longer pink inside. Serve hot or at room temperature. Makes 4 servings.

*Available at Chinese grocery stores.

*T*he richness of the black beans rounds out the Oriental flavors of these spicy wings.

Spicy Chicken Wings

3 lb	chicken wings	1.5 kg
3	cloves garlic, minced	3
1 tbsp	ground coriander	15 mL
1 tsp	ground cumin	5 mL
1 tsp	garam masala* (optional)	5 mL
1/2 tsp	hot pepper flakes	2 mL
2 tbsp	vegetable oil	25 mL
2 tbsp	vinegar	25 mL
1 tbsp	soy sauce	15 mL

● Remove tips, excess skin and fat from chicken wings; separate wings at joint and place in large bowl.

● In small bowl, combine garlic, coriander, cumin, garam masala (if using) and hot pepper flakes; stir in oil, vinegar and soy sauce. Pour over wings, turning to coat. Cover and marinate in refrigerator for at least 1 hour or up to 24 hours.

● Arrange wings on well-greased rimmed baking sheet; bake in 400°F (200°C) oven, turning once, for about 30 minutes or until no longer pink inside. Broil for 2 to 3 minutes or until crisped. Makes 4 servings.

*Available at Indian and specialty food stores.

TIP: To grease baking sheet or foil, brush lightly with vegetable oil or shortening.

*T*hese Malaysian-style wings are just as good hot or cold, making them perfect for appetizers, meals and especially picnics. Potato or rice salad, crunchy greens and sliced tomatoes round out a family-pleasing meal.

Oven-Baked Sesame Chicken Wings ▼

The secret of these irresistibly crunchy wings is the butter. For a real wing-ding feast, serve with two dips — your favorite tomato salsa, as hot as the crowd can stand it, and 2 milder sour cream dips mixed with chives or green onion and topped with crumbled blue cheese.

3 lb	chicken wings	1.5 kg
1 cup	dry bread crumbs	250 mL
1/2 cup	freshly grated Parmesan cheese	125 mL
1/3 cup	sesame seeds	75 mL
1 tsp	dried oregano	5 mL
1/2 tsp	each salt and black pepper	2 mL
1/4 tsp	cayenne pepper	1 mL
1/2 cup	butter, melted	125 mL

● Remove tips (if desired), excess skin and fat from chicken wings.

● In shallow dish, combine bread crumbs, Parmesan cheese, sesame seeds, oregano, salt, pepper and cayenne. Dip wings into butter; roll in bread crumb mixture to coat completely.

● Arrange wings, meaty side down, on well-greased rimmed baking sheet. Bake in 375°F (190°C) oven, turning halfway through, for 40 to 45 minutes or until golden, crisp and no longer pink inside. Makes 4 servings.

TIP: Save on clean-up when making wings by lining rimmed baking sheet with foil; grease foil well.

Cajun Chicken Wings

4 lb	chicken wings	2 kg
1 tbsp	vegetable oil	15 mL
1/2 cup	minced onion	125 mL
3	cloves garlic, minced	3
1 cup	chili sauce	250 mL
1/2 cup	liquid honey	125 mL
1/4 cup	cider vinegar	50 mL
1 tbsp	hot pepper sauce	15 mL
1 tbsp	horseradish	15 mL
1 tsp	liquid smoke (optional)	5 mL
1/4 tsp	each cayenne pepper, ground cloves and chili powder	1 mL

● Remove tips, excess skin and fat from chicken wings; place wings in large bowl.

● In saucepan, heat oil over medium heat; cook onion and garlic for 3 minutes or until softened. Stir in chili sauce, honey, vinegar, hot pepper sauce, horseradish, liquid smoke (if using), cayenne, cloves and chili powder; cook for 5 minutes or until bubbly. Let cool.

● Pour sauce over wings, turning to coat; cover and marinate in refrigerator for at least 12 hours or up to 24 hours.

● Reserving sauce in small saucepan, arrange wings in shallow foil-lined pan. Bake in 400°F (200°C) oven for 20 minutes.

● Meanwhile, bring sauce to boil; boil for 1 minute. Reserve 3/4 cup (175 mL) for dipping. Brush half of the remaining sauce over wings; bake, brushing with remaining sauce halfway through, for 15 minutes longer or until no longer pink inside.

● Broil wings 6 inches (15 cm) from heat for about 4 minutes or until dark golden. Transfer to warmed serving platter; serve with reserved sauce. Makes 6 servings.

Cajun, a spicy trend from the eighties, is here to stay. Even kids love the tangy nip of these Louisiana flavors — just watch how quickly a platter of these finger-lickin'-good wings disappears from the table! Serve with corn bread, rice cooked Louisiana-style with onions and sweet peppers, and a salad of greens tossed in blue cheese dressing.

Chicken Satay with Peanut Sauce

3	boneless skinless chicken breasts	3
2 tbsp	soy sauce	25 mL
2 tbsp	hoisin sauce	25 mL
1 tbsp	minced gingerroot	15 mL
1 tbsp	dry sherry	15 mL
1 tbsp	liquid honey	15 mL
1	clove garlic, minced	1
1/4 tsp	sesame oil	1 mL
	PEANUT SAUCE	
1/3 cup	coconut cream	75 mL
3 tbsp	hoisin sauce	50 mL
3 tbsp	smooth peanut butter	50 mL
4 tsp	soy sauce	20 mL
1 tbsp	minced gingerroot	15 mL
2	cloves garlic, minced	2
Dash	hot pepper sauce	Dash
2 tbsp	chopped fresh coriander	25 mL

● Cut chicken crosswise into 1/4-inch (1 cm) thick strips. In shallow baking dish, whisk together soy sauce, hoisin sauce, ginger, sherry, honey, garlic and sesame oil; add chicken and stir to coat. Cover and marinate in refrigerator for 8 hours, turning occasionally. Let stand at room temperature for 30 minutes.

● PEANUT SAUCE: Meanwhile, in small bowl, whisk together coconut cream, hoisin sauce, peanut butter, soy sauce, ginger, garlic and hot pepper sauce; stir in coriander.

● Reserving marinade, thread 3 or 4 pieces of chicken onto each of 16 soaked wooden skewers; place in single layer on foil-lined baking sheet. Broil for 3 minutes; turn and brush with marinade. Broil for 3 to 5 minutes longer or until no longer pink inside. Serve with peanut sauce. Makes 4 servings.

In summer, cook these tasty appetizers on the grill over medium-high heat. Remember to soak wooden or bamboo skewers in cold water for 30 minutes before use. Otherwise, they'll start to burn before the chicken finishes cooking.

Chicken Fingers with Plum Dipping Sauce ◄

1-1/2 cups	finely crushed soda crackers	375 mL
1/3 cup	mayonnaise	75 mL
4	boneless skinless chicken breasts	4
	PLUM DIPPING SAUCE	
3 tbsp	ketchup	50 mL
3 tbsp	plum sauce	50 mL
1 tsp	soy sauce	5 mL

● Place cracker crumbs in shallow dish. Pour mayonnaise into bowl. Cut each chicken breast crosswise into 4 or 5 strips; pat dry.

● Add chicken to mayonnaise, turning to coat all over. One at a time, transfer chicken strips to cracker crumbs, patting crumbs all over chicken.

● Arrange chicken in single layer on well-greased rimmed baking sheet. Bake in 400°F (200°C) oven for 15 minutes. Turn strips over and bake for 10 to 12 minutes longer or until golden and no longer pink inside.

● PLUM DIPPING SAUCE: Meanwhile, in small bowl, stir together ketchup, plum sauce and soy sauce. Place in center of serving platter; arrange chicken strips around bowl. Makes 4 servings.

TIP: To crush crackers, whiz in food processor, or enclose in large bag and roll with a rolling pin until crackers are in fine crumbs.

When you and your children see how easy it is to make your own crisp-on-the-outside, juicy-on-the-inside chicken fingers, you'll never settle for the fast food ones again.
A great recipe to get kids cooking in the kitchen!

Chicken Liver Pâté

1 lb	chicken livers	500 g
1/3 cup	butter	75 mL
1	small onion, chopped	1
1	small apple, peeled, cored and chopped	1
1/2 cup	dry white wine	125 mL
1	bay leaf	1
1 tsp	salt	5 mL
1/2 tsp	each pepper and dry mustard	2 mL
1/2 tsp	dried thyme	2 mL
2 tbsp	light cream	25 mL
2 tsp	brandy	10 mL

● Trim livers; cut in half. Set aside.

● In skillet, melt 2 tbsp (25 mL) of the butter over medium-high heat; cook onion, stirring, for 3 minutes. Stir in apple and wine; cook, stirring, for 5 minutes or until apple has

softened and wine has evaporated. Transfer to blender.

● In same skillet, melt 2 tbsp (25 mL) of the remaining butter. Stir in bay leaf, salt, pepper, mustard and thyme; cook, stirring, for 1 minute. Add chicken livers; cook for 8 minutes or until browned but still slightly pink inside. Discard bay leaf. Transfer mixture to blender.

● Pour in cream; purée until smooth. Press through fine sieve into bowl; let cool slightly.

● Using wooden spoon, beat in remaining butter; mix in brandy. Pack into 2-cup (500 mL) mould lined with plastic wrap. Cover with plastic wrap and refrigerate for at least 4 hours or up to 2 days. Makes 2 cups (500 mL).

Chicken liver pâté should be luxurious, but some pâtés are more butter than liver. Here's a nicely balanced one — creamy but not too rich, and utterly divine on melba toast. It's quick to make, too.

Peanutty Chicken Pitas ▲

Grilled chicken drizzled with tangy peanut sauce comes nicely packaged in a pita with sprouts, cucumber and tomato — perfect for summertime eating.

2	boneless skinless chicken breasts	2
Pinch	each salt and pepper	Pinch
1/3 cup	smooth peanut butter	75 mL
2	cloves garlic, minced	2
2 tbsp	chopped fresh coriander or parsley	25 mL
1 tbsp	minced gingerroot	15 mL
1 tbsp	sweet mustard	15 mL
4 tsp	soy sauce	20 mL
2 tsp	white wine vinegar	10 mL
1/4 cup	(approx) warm water	50 mL
2	pita breads	2
4	lettuce leaves	4
1-1/2 cups	alfalfa sprouts	375 mL
1/2 cup	chopped cucumber	125 mL
1	tomato, diced	1
2	green onions, chopped	2

● Sprinkle chicken with salt and pepper. Place on greased grill over medium-high heat; cook, turning once, for 12 minutes or until no longer pink inside. Let cool slightly; slice into strips.

● Meanwhile, in small bowl, whisk together peanut butter, garlic, coriander, ginger, mustard, soy sauce, vinegar and water until smooth and consistency of yogurt, adding up to 1 tbsp (15 mL) more water if too thick.

● Cut pitas in half; open to form pockets. Line inside of each with lettuce leaf and alfalfa sprouts. Divide chicken, cucumber and tomato among pitas. Spoon 2 tbsp (25 mL) sauce into each; sprinkle with green onions. Pass remaining sauce separately. Makes 4 servings.

Chicken Mushroom Calzone

2 tbsp	granulated sugar	25 mL
3 cups	warm water	750 mL
2	pkg active dry yeast (or 2 tbsp/25 mL)	2
2-1/2 cups	whole wheat flour	625 mL
3 tbsp	olive oil	50 mL
1 tbsp	salt	15 mL
5 cups	all-purpose flour	1.25 L
1	egg, beaten	1
	FILLING	
1 lb	ground chicken	500 g
4 cups	sliced mushrooms	1 L
1 tsp	each dried basil and pepper	5 mL
3/4 tsp	salt	4 mL
1/2 tsp	dried thyme	2 mL
2 cups	shredded mozzarella cheese	500 mL
2 cups	All-Purpose Tomato Sauce (recipe follows)	500 mL
1 cup	freshly grated Parmesan cheese	250 mL
2	green onions, chopped	2

● In large bowl, dissolve sugar in water; sprinkle yeast over top and let stand for 10 minutes or until frothy.

● Using electric mixer, beat in whole wheat flour, oil and salt. Using wooden spoon, beat in enough of the all-purpose flour to make moderately stiff dough.

● Turn out dough onto lightly floured surface; knead for about 10 minutes or until smooth and elastic. Place in greased bowl, turning to grease all over. Cover and let rise for 1-1/2 hours or until doubled in bulk.

● FILLING: Meanwhile, in Dutch oven, cook chicken over high heat, stirring to break up meat, for 3 to 4 minutes or until no longer pink. Stir in mushrooms; cook, stirring, for 7 to 9 minutes or until liquid has evaporated. Stir in basil, pepper, salt and thyme; cook for 30 seconds. Remove from heat; stir in mozzarella, tomato sauce, Parmesan and onions.

● Punch down dough; divide into 12 portions. On lightly floured surface, roll out each into 8-inch (20 cm) circle. Spread 1/2 cup (125 mL) filling over half of circle; moisten edge of dough with water and fold uncovered edge over, pressing to seal. Using handle of wooden spoon, crimp pastry edge every 1/2 inch (1 cm).

● Transfer to lightly floured baking sheet; cover with damp cloth and let stand for 30 minutes. Crimp edges again if necessary. Prick calzone; brush with egg. Bake in 400°F (200°C) oven for 30 minutes or until golden and sounds hollow when tapped on bottom. Makes 12 calzone.

	ALL-PURPOSE TOMATO SAUCE	
2 tbsp	olive oil	25 mL
2	onions, chopped	2
4	cloves garlic, minced	4
1 tbsp	paprika	15 mL
2 tsp	dried basil	10 mL
1 tsp	each dried oregano and salt	5 mL
1/2 tsp	each dried thyme and pepper	2 mL
5	carrots, grated	5
2	stalks celery, chopped	2
2	sweet green peppers, chopped	2
3	cans (each 28 oz/796 mL) stewed tomatoes	3
1 cup	tomato paste	250 mL
1/4 cup	chopped fresh parsley	50 mL

● In large heavy saucepan, heat oil over medium heat; cook onions and garlic for 3 minutes or until softened. Stir in paprika, basil, oregano, salt, thyme and pepper; cook, stirring, for 30 seconds. Add carrots, celery and green peppers; cook, stirring occasionally, for 3 minutes. Add tomatoes and tomato paste; bring to boil. Reduce heat to medium-low and cook, stirring occasionally, for 2 hours. Stir in parsley. Makes 12 cups (3 L).

Golden bread wraps a chicken and mushroom filling in this meal-in-a-mitt. Calzone are also great stuff for a teen bash or casual get-together. Serve them as is, or use the versatile dough for an instant pizza base (see below). However you enjoy calzone, make sure you have plenty of All-Purpose Tomato Sauce on hand or in the freezer as a topper.

FROM CALZONE TO PIZZA

Turn the versatile calzone dough into pizza bases. Simply roll the dough into four 12-inch (30 cm) circles and transfer to pizza pans. Top with 1 cup (250 mL) All-Purpose Tomato Sauce or spaghetti sauce, your favorite fixings and cheese and bake in 400°F (200°C) oven for 10 minutes or until golden, puffed and bubbling.

New Chicken Club

A classic gets a nineties taste lift with crunchy sprouts and a hit of Dijon mustard.

8	slices whole wheat bread	8
1/4 cup	light mayonnaise	50 mL
8	thin slices tomato	8
	Salt and pepper	
8	slices cooked chicken	8
6	lettuce leaves	6
2 tbsp	Dijon mustard	25 mL
4	slices bacon, cooked	4
2/3 cup	alfalfa sprouts	150 mL

● Toast bread; spread 1 slice with 1-1/2 tsp (7 mL) mayonnaise. Top with 2 slices tomato; sprinkle with salt and pepper to taste. Top with 2 thin slices chicken, then 1 lettuce leaf.

● Spread 1-1/2 tsp (7 mL) mustard over second slice and place, mustard side down, over lettuce; spread with 1-1/2 tsp (7 mL) mayonnaise. Cut 2 slices of bacon in half; lay on top. Top with half of the alfalfa sprouts and another lettuce leaf.

● Spread 1-1/2 tsp (7 mL) mustard over third slice; place, mustard side down, on lettuce. Spread with 1-1/2 tsp (7 mL) mayonnaise.

● Repeat layering with tomatoes, chicken, lettuce and mayonnaise-covered toast. Place toothpicks through sandwich; cut into quarters. Repeat for second sandwich. Makes 2 to 4 servings.

Grilled Chicken Sandwich

One of the best things about cooking in recent years has been the exciting taste difference that grilling brings to everyday food. Here, grilled chicken totally transforms ho-hum lunchy sandwiches into fun supper food.

2	boneless skinless chicken breasts	2
1 tbsp	olive oil	15 mL
1/2 tsp	dried basil	2 mL
8	slices whole wheat bread	8
3 tbsp	light mayonnaise	50 mL
1 tsp	lemon juice	5 mL
4	lettuce leaves	4
4	thin slices red onion	4
4	pieces roasted red pepper	4
1	avocado, sliced	1
	Salt and pepper	

● Pound chicken lightly; brush with oil and sprinkle with basil. Cook on greased grill over medium-high heat, turning once, for 12 to 14 minutes or until no longer pink inside. Let cool slightly. Cut each breast in half horizontally to cover slice of bread.

● Grill one side of bread for 1 to 2 minutes or until lightly toasted. Combine mayonnaise with lemon juice; spread 1 tsp (5 mL) on untoasted side of each piece of bread.

● Layer lettuce, onion, chicken, red pepper and avocado evenly among 4 slices of bread; season with salt and pepper to taste. Top with remaining bread. Makes 4 servings.

COOKED CHICKEN ON STANDBY

Having cooked chicken on hand in the refrigerator and ready for sandwiches and salads makes mealtime quick and easy. Here's how to cook 2 boneless skinless chicken breasts (about 4 oz/125 g each) until no longer pink inside. Refrigerate cooked chicken immediately and use within two days.

● **Panfry**: 15 minutes over medium heat in lightly greased pan.

● **Poach**: 15 minutes in simmering water or chicken stock.

● **Microwave**: 6 minutes at High.

● **Bake**: 20 minutes in 375°F (190°C) oven.

● **Grill**: 15 minutes, covered and turning once, over medium-high heat.

Souvlakia with Tzatziki ▲

6	boneless skinless chicken breasts	6
1/4 cup	olive oil	50 mL
2 tbsp	lemon juice	25 mL
1 tsp	dried oregano	5 mL
1/2 tsp	each ground cumin and coriander	2 mL
1/2 tsp	salt	2 mL
1/4 tsp	each pepper and hot pepper flakes	1 mL
2	cloves garlic, minced	2
8	pita breads	8
	TZATZIKI SAUCE	
1	small English cucumber	1
1 tsp	salt	5 mL
1-1/2 cups	plain yogurt	375 mL
2 tbsp	chopped fresh mint	25 mL
2 tbsp	chopped fresh coriander or parsley	25 mL
2	cloves garlic, minced	2
1/2 tsp	hot pepper sauce	2 mL
1	sweet green pepper, finely diced	1
	Salt and pepper	

● Cut chicken into 2-inch (5 cm) chunks; pat dry with paper towels. In bowl, combine oil, lemon juice, oregano, cumin, coriander, salt, pepper, hot pepper flakes and garlic. Add chicken and stir to coat; cover and marinate in refrigerator for 2 hours. Let stand at room temperature for 30 minutes.

● TZATZIKI SAUCE: Quarter cucumber lengthwise; slice crosswise. Toss with salt; let drain for 30 minutes in colander set over bowl. Discard liquid and pat cucumber dry. In fine-mesh sieve set over bowl, drain yogurt for 30 minutes; discard liquid. In bowl, combine cucumber, yogurt, mint, coriander, garlic, hot pepper sauce, green pepper, and salt and pepper to taste.

● Thread chicken pieces onto metal skewers. Broil or place on greased grill over medium-high heat; cook, turning every 3 or 4 minutes, for 10 to 12 minutes or until no longer pink inside.

● Cut pitas in half; open to form pockets. Slide chicken off skewers into pita pockets; top with sauce. Makes 8 sandwiches.

Serve this Greek kabob in toasted sesame buns or pita halves, and provide extra bread for mopping up the irresistible yogurt sauce.

TIP: Tzatziki is also delicious on its own as a dip with pita triangles, or drizzled over grilled chicken, fish and pork.

International Flavors

Let chicken be your passport to a world of new flavors. From exotic tandoori to hot new Thai or never-out-of-style Italian, globetrotting has never been tastier!

Spicy Szechuan Chicken Stir-Fry ◄

3	boneless skinless chicken breasts	3
6	green onions	6
2	sweet green or red peppers	2
1	onion	1
3	cloves garlic, minced	3
1 tbsp	grated gingerroot	15 mL
1	small hot chili pepper, minced (optional)	1
1/2 cup	orange juice	125 mL
2 tbsp	soy sauce	25 mL
1 tbsp	each sherry, hoisin sauce and sesame oil	15 mL
2 tsp	cider vinegar	10 mL
1 tsp	granulated sugar	5 mL
1 tsp	Chinese chili paste	5 mL
2 tsp	cornstarch	10 mL
2 tbsp	cold water	25 mL
2 tbsp	peanut or vegetable oil	25 mL
1 tbsp	grated orange rind	15 mL
1/3 cup	each chopped peanuts and green onions	75 mL

● Slice chicken across the grain into thin strips; set aside. Diagonally slice green onions into 1-inch (2.5 cm) lengths. Cut green peppers and onion into 3/4-inch (2 cm) chunks. Set aside.

● In small dish, combine garlic, ginger, and hot pepper (if using). In small bowl, combine orange juice, soy sauce, sherry, hoisin sauce, sesame oil, vinegar, sugar and chili paste. In another small dish, stir cornstarch into water until dissolved.

● Heat wok or large skillet over high heat for 1 minute; add 1 tbsp (15 mL) of the oil and swirl to coat wok. Stir-fry chicken for 3 minutes or until no longer pink inside; remove and set aside.

● Heat remaining oil in wok; stir-fry green onions, green peppers and onion for 3 minutes or until tender-crisp. Add garlic mixture; stir-fry for 1 minute.

● Return chicken to wok; add orange juice mixture and stir-fry for 2 minutes. Stir in orange rind and cornstarch mixture; stir-fry for 1 minute or until sauce is thickened and clear. Garnish with peanuts and chopped green onions. Makes 4 servings.

This beautifully balanced dish — with accents of orange and green onion, and tingles of hot pepper — will renew your appetite for stir-frys. Nice with rice, it's even better with Chinese noodles. Look for them in Oriental grocery stores and some supermarkets.

Italian Devilled Chicken

A *split plump fryer gets a zippy mustard and bread coating for a classic diàvolo touch. Serve with a radish and watercress salad, Italian bread and oven-fried potato wedges.*

1	chicken (3 lb/1.5 kg), halved	1
1	large lemon, halved	1
1 tsp	coarse salt	5 mL
1/3 cup	Dijon mustard	75 mL
3 tbsp	freshly grated Parmesan cheese	50 mL
2 tbsp	packed brown sugar	25 mL
2 tbsp	butter, softened	25 mL
2	cloves garlic, minced	2
1/4 tsp	cayenne pepper	1 mL
1/4 cup	dry bread crumbs	50 mL

● Stretch out each chicken half by pulling to elongate and flatten; tuck wing tips under. Rub both sides of each half with lemon; place in shallow dish and sprinkle with salt. Refrigerate, skin side up and uncovered, for 4 hours. Let stand at room temperature for 30 minutes.

● Place, skin side down, in shallow foil-lined pan; broil 4 inches (10 cm) from heat for 10 minutes or until golden. Turn and broil for 4 to 8 minutes or until golden.

● Combine mustard, Parmesan, sugar, butter, garlic and cayenne; spread over chicken. Sprinkle with bread crumbs.

● Bake in 450°F (230°C) oven for 12 to 15 minutes or until dark golden and juices run clear when chicken is pierced. Transfer to platter and let stand for 10 minutes; divide into 4 portions to serve. Makes 4 servings.

HOW TO HALVE A CHICKEN

● Poultry shears are worth their weight in gold when it comes to dividing a chicken into parts. Sturdy kitchen shears work well, too, and even a good sharp knife can be used as long as the blade is not too long or flexible.

1 Place chicken, breast down, on cutting board. Trim off and discard any visible fat at cavity and neck.

2 Using a kitchen towel to prevent slipping, grasp chicken firmly with the hand that is not holding the scissors. Starting at the body cavity end, cut as closely as possible along both sides of backbone.

3 Turn chicken over; open up slightly and cut in half through middle of breast-bone. Cut off wing tips.

4 Store wing tips and backbone in freezer bags in freezer to make chicken stock (recipe, p. 44).

HOW TO CUT UP A CHICKEN

● Cutting up a chicken is a simple and easy way to save money. You'll end up with 8 or 10 portions, plus back-bone, neck, wing tips and giblets for chicken stock.

1 Cut chicken in half, as above. Lay chicken halves, skin side up, on board. Lift legs, one at a time, cutting through skin and meat to separate leg from body.

2 Bend back thigh and drumstick until joint pops. Cut through skin and meat at joint.

3 Divide each breast and wing into two portions by cutting across from breast diagonally about an inch (2.5 cm) below the wing joint, allowing each portion equal amounts of the high-quality white meat.

● A more conventional way of cutting this part of the chicken is to remove the wings, leaving only the breasts. To do so, cut around the joint joining the wing to the breast. Trim off excess skin from chicken pieces; discard any shards of bones.

Greek Chicken Stifado ▲

1 tbsp	olive oil	15 mL
1	chicken, cut into 8 pieces	1
Pinch	each salt and pepper	Pinch
1	onion, slivered	1
2	sweet red peppers, slivered	2
2	cloves garlic, slivered	2
1	can (28 oz/796 mL) stewed tomatoes	1
1/2 cup	Kalamata or other black olives	125 mL
1/3 cup	dried currants	75 mL
1 tbsp	drained capers	15 mL
1 tbsp	lemon juice	15 mL
1 tsp	each dried oregano and mint	5 mL
	Gremolada (recipe follows)	

● In large skillet, heat oil over medium-high heat; cook chicken, in batches, for about 5 minutes or until browned. Arrange, skin side up, in 13- x 9-inch (3.5 L) baking dish; sprinkle with salt and pepper. Set aside.

● Pour off all but 1 tbsp (15 mL) drippings from skillet; cook onion, red peppers and garlic over medium heat for 5 minutes or until softened. Spoon over chicken.

● To skillet, add tomatoes, olives, currants, capers, lemon juice, oregano and mint; bring to boil. Reduce heat and simmer, stirring occasionally, for 15 minutes or until thickened; pour over chicken.

● Bake, uncovered, in 350°F (180°C) oven for 50 to 55 minutes or until juices run clear when chicken is pierced. Sprinkle with Gremolada. Makes 6 servings.

GREMOLADA		
1/3 cup	minced fresh parsley	75 mL
2 tbsp	grated lemon rind	25 mL
2 tbsp	minced fresh dill	25 mL
3	cloves garlic, minced	3

● Combine parsley, lemon rind, dill and garlic; cover and refrigerate for up to 3 hours. Makes 2/3 cup (150 mL).

Studded with currants, capers and olives, this savory braised chicken is an easy-to-make entertaining dish. Carry out the Greek theme with orzo (rice-shaped pasta) or rice, grilled pita bread and a salad of lettuce, tomatoes and cucumbers sprinkled with oregano and crumbled feta cheese.

Antipasto Chicken Spirals

Stuffing and rolling chicken breasts may seem fiddly, but these Italian-inspired ones from Toronto's ever-popular Grano restaurant are truly worth the effort. Slice them thinly as part of an antipasto platter or serve them hot and whole as a dinner party entrée.

1	peeled roasted sweet red pepper (see TIP, this page)	1
Half	pkg (10 oz/284 g) spinach, trimmed	Half
1/4 cup	freshly grated Parmesan cheese	50 mL
2	cloves garlic, minced	2
6	large boneless skinless chicken breasts	6
2 tbsp	olive oil	25 mL
12	thin slices prosciutto ham (8 oz/250 g)	12
6	very thin slices fontina or mozzarella cheese	6

TIP: Roast red pepper on baking sheet in 375°F (190°C) oven, turning often, for 30 to 35 minutes or until puffed and browned. Let cool and peel.

● Cut red pepper lengthwise into 1/2-inch (1 cm) wide strips; set aside.

● Rinse spinach; shake off excess water. Place in saucepan with just the water clinging to leaves; cover and cook over medium-high heat for 2 minutes or just until wilted. Drain and press out moisture; chop finely and combine with Parmesan and garlic.

● Lay chicken flat, placing filet to side of breast. Brush with 1 tbsp (15 mL) of the oil. Over each breast, layer prosciutto and fontina cheese. Arrange red pepper strips along center of 3 of the breasts; arrange spinach mixture on remaining breasts.

● Starting at long side, roll up chicken, tucking in ends; wrap each in foil to make sausage-shaped roll. Bake on baking sheet in 375°F (190°C) oven for 15 to 20 minutes or until no longer pink inside. Let stand for 5 minutes; remove foil.

● Brush rolls with remaining oil. Broil or grill for 3 to 4 minutes or until attractively marked. Let cool. Cut into slices. Makes 36 slices.

Italian Ricotta-Stuffed Chicken Breasts

These chicken breasts — stuffed with ricotta, basil, pine nuts and sun-dried tomatoes — are worthy of any special occasion. Serve them over spinach pasta to show off the tomato sauce.

1/3 cup	dry-packed sun-dried tomatoes	75 mL
3/4 cup	low-fat ricotta cheese	175 mL
1/2 cup	chopped fresh basil	125 mL
1/4 cup	freshly grated Parmesan cheese	50 mL
1/4 cup	lightly toasted pine nuts or chopped almonds	50 mL
	Pepper	
8	boneless skinless chicken breasts	8
1 tbsp	olive oil	15 mL
1/2 cup	white wine or chicken stock	125 mL
2	cloves garlic, minced	2
4	tomatoes, peeled, seeded and diced	4
	Salt	

● In bowl, soak dried tomatoes in boiling water for 10 minutes. Drain and chop finely; place in bowl. Mix in ricotta, half of the basil, the Parmesan, nuts, and pepper to taste.

● Between plastic wrap, pound chicken to flatten to 1/4-inch (5 mm) thickness. Spread each with 2 tbsp (25 mL) ricotta mixture, leaving 1/2-inch (1 cm) border; roll up from narrow end, securing with toothpick.

● In large nonstick skillet, heat oil over medium-high heat; cook chicken for 5 to 7 minutes or until lightly browned. Arrange in 13- x 9-inch (3 L) baking dish.

● Add wine and garlic to skillet; bring to boil over high heat. Cook for 2 minutes or until almost evaporated. Add tomatoes; cook, stirring, for 5 to 8 minutes or until thickened. Add remaining basil; season with salt and pepper to taste. Spoon over rolls.

● Bake, covered, in 350°F (180°C) oven for 30 to 35 minutes or until no longer pink inside. Remove toothpicks. Serve with sauce. Makes 8 servings.

Sunny Chicken Paella ▼

4	chicken legs	4
1 tsp	salt	5 mL
1/2 tsp	pepper	2 mL
1 tbsp	olive or vegetable oil	15 mL
2	onions, chopped	2
4	cloves garlic, minced	4
1 tbsp	paprika	15 mL
3/4 tsp	turmeric	4 mL
Pinch	cayenne pepper	Pinch
1	can (19 oz/540 mL) tomatoes	1
3 cups	chicken stock	750 mL
2 cups	long grain rice	500 mL
1	sweet red pepper, cut into strips	1
1 cup	fresh or frozen peas	250 mL

● Separate chicken legs at joint; sprinkle with 1/4 tsp (1 mL) each of the salt and pepper.

● In large deep skillet, heat oil over medium heat; cook chicken, turning once, for 20 minutes or until golden brown. Remove and set aside.

● Drain fat from skillet. Cook onions and garlic, stirring, for 3 minutes. Add paprika, turmeric, cayenne and remaining salt and pepper; cook, stirring, for 30 seconds.

● Coarsely chop tomatoes and add along with juice to skillet, stirring to scrape up brown bits. Add stock and rice; bring to boil.

● Return chicken to skillet; reduce heat, cover and simmer for 30 minutes or until juices run clear when chicken is pierced and rice is just tender. Stir in red pepper and peas; cover and cook for 10 to 15 minutes or until liquid is absorbed. Makes 6 servings.

This variation on a classic paella is easier to make and concentrates on one of its great ingredients — chicken.

Spicy Coconut Chicken ▼

It's well worth setting aside time to put together the marinade and chicken for this impressive Southeast Asian-inspired dish. Then, when company comes, the cooking is easy. Serve with rice and roasted vegetables.

1/2 cup	toasted walnuts, finely chopped	125 mL	1 tsp	salt	5 mL
1/2 cup	minced fresh coriander	125 mL	1/4 tsp	ground cumin	1 mL
2 tbsp	curry powder	25 mL	1 cup	coconut milk	250 mL
2 tbsp	packed brown sugar	25 mL	1/3 cup	fish sauce	75 mL
10	cloves garlic, minced	10	1/4 cup	lime juice	50 mL
1 tbsp	finely chopped fresh lemongrass	15 mL	2 tbsp	rye whisky	25 mL
2 tsp	hot pepper flakes	10 mL	8	chicken legs	8
			1	orange, thinly sliced	1

● In large bowl, stir together walnuts, coriander, curry powder, sugar, garlic, lemongrass, hot pepper flakes, salt and cumin; mix in coconut milk, fish sauce, lime juice and whisky.

● Add chicken, turning to coat. Cover and marinate in refrigerator for at least 8 hours or up to 1 day, turning occasionally. Let stand at room temperature for 30 minutes.

● Reserving marinade, arrange chicken on rack on rimmed baking sheet. Bake in 375°F (190°C) oven for 25 minutes; brush with marinade. Bake for 15 to 25 minutes longer or until juices run clear when chicken is pierced. Garnish with orange slices. Makes 8 servings.

Not Quite Tandoori Chicken

6	chicken legs	6
1-1/2 cups	plain yogurt	375 mL
2 tbsp	cornstarch	25 mL
2	cloves garlic, minced	2
1 tbsp	grated gingerroot	15 mL
1 tbsp	curry powder	15 mL
3/4 tsp	each ground coriander, cumin and turmeric	4 mL
3/4 tsp	each hot pepper flakes, paprika and salt	4 mL
3/4 tsp	packed brown sugar	4 mL
1/2 tsp	cayenne pepper	2 mL

● Remove skin from chicken; cut 1/8-inch (3 mm) deep cuts, 1 inch (2.5 cm) apart, diagonally across meaty sides. Arrange, meaty side up, in 13- x 9-inch (3 L) glass baking dish.

● Whisk together yogurt, cornstarch, garlic, ginger, curry powder, coriander, cumin, turmeric, hot pepper flakes, paprika, salt, sugar and cayenne pepper; pour over chicken. Cover and marinate in refrigerator for 24 hours, turning occasionally. Let stand at room temperature for 30 minutes.

● Arrange chicken on foil-lined rimmed baking sheet, leaving space between pieces and covering each with sauce. Bake in 425°F (220°C) oven for 35 minutes or until golden and juices run clear when chicken is pierced. Broil 6 inches (15 cm) from heat for about 2 minutes or until crisp. Makes 6 servings.

This is as close as you can get with a home stove to the spicy chicken cooked in the intense heat of an authentic tandoor oven. Serve with Basmati rice, a cool cucumber yogurt salad and mango chutney.

Teriyaki Chicken with Tropical Salsa

2 tbsp	low-sodium soy sauce	25 mL
1/4 tsp	each granulated sugar and ginger	1 mL
2	cloves garlic, crushed	2
4	boneless skinless chicken breasts	4
	TROPICAL SALSA	
1	small mango, peeled and diced	1
1	kiwifruit, peeled and diced	1
2 tbsp	rice wine vinegar or white wine vinegar	25 mL
1	banana, diced	1
1	green onion, sliced	1
2 tbsp	diced sweet red pepper	25 mL
	Salt, pepper and hot pepper flakes	

● In shallow dish, combine soy sauce, sugar, ginger and garlic; add chicken, turning to coat. Cover and marinate at room temperature for 20 minutes or in refrigerator for up to 8 hours. Remove from refrigerator 30 minutes before cooking.

● TROPICAL SALSA: Just before cooking chicken, combine mango, kiwifruit and vinegar. Stir in banana, green onion, red pepper, and salt, pepper and hot pepper flakes to taste.

● Broil chicken 6 inches (15 cm) from heat, turning once, for about 12 minutes or until no longer pink inside. Serve with Tropical Salsa. Makes 2 servings.

While the chicken is marinating, make the colorful salsa and put a pot of rice on to cook. In warm weather, you can grill the chicken.

SAY SI TO SALSA!

Salsa is a low-fat way to add extra flavor and moistness to a dish. The fresh kind is simply a combo of vegetables or fruit with a sour touch such as lime juice or vinegar and a hit of hot from peppers. Fresh coriander adds its own pungency to the mix. Salsa, which is simply "sauce" in Spanish, can also be a cooked tomato-based chunky sauce that now outsells ketchup.

Thai Barbecued Chicken ▶

Eating this Thai meal is simple and encourages a relaxed and friendly spirit around the table. Just place some vegetables from the Thai Vegetable Platter (this page) on a lettuce leaf along with a piece of the golden-skinned chicken, roll into a slim bundle, dip into Sweet and Sour Sauce and pop into your mouth. Golden Thread Fried Rice (recipe, p. 72) is a satisfying accompaniment.

2 tbsp	fish sauce or light soy sauce	25 mL
1 tbsp	lemon juice	15 mL
1 tbsp	vegetable oil	15 mL
2	cloves garlic, minced	2
2 tsp	turmeric	10 mL
1/2 tsp	salt	2 mL
1/4 tsp	granulated sugar	1 mL
6	boneless chicken breasts	6
Half	sweet red pepper, cut into strips	Half
6	sprigs fresh coriander	6
	Sweet and Sour Sauce (recipe follows)	

● In large bowl, combine fish sauce, lemon juice, oil, garlic, turmeric, salt and sugar. Add chicken, turning to coat. Cover and marinate in refrigerator for at least 8 hours or up to 24 hours. Let stand at room temperature for 30 minutes.

● Place chicken, skin side up, on rimmed baking sheet; bake in 350°F (180°C) oven for 20 minutes or until no longer pink inside. Broil for 2 to 4 minutes or until crispy and browned.

● Cut chicken crosswise into 1/2-inch (1 cm) thick pieces. Arrange on platter; garnish with red pepper and coriander. Serve with bowls of Sweet and Sour Sauce. Makes 6 servings.

SWEET AND SOUR SAUCE		
2 cups	water	500 mL
1-1/2 cups	granulated sugar	375 mL
Half	sweet red pepper (seeds and membrane intact), chopped	Half
1/3 cup	lemon juice	75 mL
2	cloves garlic	2
3 tbsp	fish sauce or light soy sauce	50 mL
1 tsp	salt	5 mL
	Hot pepper sauce	
2 tbsp	finely chopped peanuts	25 mL

● In saucepan, bring water and sugar to boil over high heat; boil for 10 minutes. Let cool completely.

● In food processor or blender, purée 1/2 cup (125 mL) of the sugar syrup, red pepper, lemon juice, garlic, fish sauce and salt (pepper seeds will remain intact). Stir into remaining sugar syrup; add hot pepper sauce to taste. *(Sauce can be covered and refrigerated for up to 4 weeks.)*

● To serve, pour into individual bowls; sprinkle with chopped peanuts. Makes about 2 cups (500 mL).

Thai Vegetable Platter ▶

Start with your prettiest platter or tray, and this simple arrangement of fresh colorful vegetables becomes a work of art.

1	large head leaf lettuce, separated	1
1 cup	sliced English cucumber	250 mL
2	tomatoes, sliced	2
1 cup	finely shredded red cabbage	250 mL
1 cup	mung bean sprouts	250 mL
Half	bunch fresh coriander or watercress	Half
1	bunch fresh mint (optional)	1

● On large platter, arrange lettuce leaves, cucumber, tomatoes, cabbage, bean sprouts, coriander, and mint (if using) in overlapping piles. Cover and refrigerate for up to 1 hour. Makes 6 servings.

*Thai Vegetable Platter with Thai Barbecued Chicken.
(at top) Golden Thread Fried Rice (p. 72) and bowls of Sweet and Sour Sauce.*

Golden Thread Fried Rice

Golden threads of fried egg transform rice into a special-occasion dish (photo, p. 71). Serve with Thai Barbecued Chicken (previous page).

3 tbsp	vegetable oil	50 mL
3	cloves garlic, minced	3
3 cups	cold cooked rice	750 mL
2 tbsp	fish sauce or light soy sauce	25 mL
1 tbsp	oyster sauce	15 mL
1/2 tsp	pepper	2 mL
2	green onions, thinly sliced	2
1	tomato, diced	1
	GOLDEN THREADS	
3	eggs	3
2 tbsp	water	25 mL
1 tbsp	vegetable oil	15 mL

● GOLDEN THREADS: Beat eggs with water until well blended. In nonstick 8-inch (20 cm) skillet, heat 1 tsp (5 mL) of the oil over medium heat. Pour in one-third of the egg mixture, swirling to coat skillet. Reduce heat to low; cover and cook for 30 seconds or until set. Slide onto plate. Repeat with remaining egg mixture and oil, stacking egg sheets. Let cool and cut into 1/8-inch (3 mm) wide strips; set aside.

● In large skillet or wok, heat oil over high heat; cook garlic for 30 seconds or until golden. Add rice, stirring to coat.

● Stir in fish sauce, oyster sauce and pepper. Reduce heat to low; cover and cook, stirring occasionally, for 3 to 5 minutes or until heated through. Stir in green onions, tomato and reserved Golden Threads. Makes 6 servings.

Singapore Noodles with Chicken

Curry is the definitive flavor in this big wokfull of noodles, vegetables and chicken. Garnish serving platter with additional chopped green onions.

8 oz	rice vermicelli	250 g
1/3 cup	soy sauce	75 mL
3 tbsp	packed brown sugar	50 mL
3 tbsp	rice wine vinegar	50 mL
2 tbsp	oyster sauce	25 mL
1 tbsp	cornstarch	15 mL
3 tbsp	vegetable oil	50 mL
1 tbsp	curry powder	15 mL
1 tbsp	minced gingerroot	15 mL
2	cloves garlic, minced	2
3	green onions, chopped	3
3	boneless skinless chicken breasts, cut into strips	3
8 oz	raw shrimp, peeled and deveined	250 g
1	each sweet red and green pepper, cut crosswise and julienned	1
4 oz	snow peas, trimmed	125 g
1	carrot, sliced on diagonal	1

● In bowl, cover rice vermicelli with hot water; let stand for 20 minutes. Drain well.

● Meanwhile, whisk together soy sauce, sugar, vinegar, oyster sauce and cornstarch; set aside.

● In wok, heat oil over medium-high heat; stir-fry curry powder, ginger, garlic and green onions for 30 seconds. Add chicken and shrimp; stir-fry for about 5 minutes or until chicken is no longer pink inside and shrimp are pink.

● Add red and green peppers, snow peas, carrot and sauce mixture; cover and cook for 2 minutes. Add noodles; toss to coat well and heat through. Makes 4 servings.

Chicken and Egg Pad Thai

1	pkg (227 g) wide rice noodles	1
2/3 cup	chicken stock	150 mL
1/2 cup	ketchup	125 mL
1/4 cup	fish sauce	50 mL
1 tsp	lime rind	5 mL
1/4 cup	lime juice	50 mL
2 tbsp	granulated sugar	25 mL
4 tsp	cornstarch	20 mL
1/2 tsp	hot pepper sauce	2 mL
6 oz	firm tofu	175 g
2	boneless skinless chicken breasts	2
3 tbsp	vegetable oil	45 mL
3	eggs, lightly beaten	3
3	cloves garlic, minced	3
2 tsp	minced gingerroot	10 mL
2	carrots, grated	2
1	sweet red pepper, chopped	1
1 cup	bean sprouts	250 mL
6	green onions, chopped	6
1/4 cup	chopped peanuts	50 mL
1/4 cup	chopped fresh coriander	50 mL

● In large bowl, soak noodles in warm water for 15 minutes; drain and set aside.

● Meanwhile, whisk together stock, ketchup, fish sauce, lime rind and juice, sugar, cornstarch and hot pepper sauce; set aside.

● Cut tofu into 1/2-inch (1 cm) cubes. Cut chicken into 1/4-inch (5 mm) thick strips.

● In wok or large skillet, heat 1 tbsp (15 mL) of the oil over medium heat; cook eggs, stirring occasionally, for 3 minutes or until scrambled and set. Transfer to plate.

● Wipe out wok; add 1 tbsp (15 mL) of the remaining oil. Stir-fry garlic, ginger and chicken over medium-high heat for about 5 minutes or until chicken is no longer pink inside. Add to egg.

● Add remaining oil to wok. Stir in tofu, carrots and red pepper; cook, stirring occasionally, for 2 minutes or until tofu begins to brown.

● Add noodles; stir gently for about 1 minute or until beginning to wilt. Stir sauce and pour into wok; stir-fry gently for 3 minutes or until noodles are tender.

● Return egg mixture to wok; add bean sprouts and half of the green onions. Toss gently for 2 to 3 minutes or until heated through. Remove to serving platter; garnish with peanuts, remaining green onions and coriander. Makes 4 servings.

Pad Thai is Thailand's answer to macaroni and cheese or spaghetti and ragu sauce. This noodle, shrimp, vegetable and chicken combo is a symphony of flavors, easy to eat and so easy to like.

STORING CHICKEN

● As soon as chicken is unpacked from grocery bags, place packages on tray and store in coldest part of refrigerator (40°F/4°C), usually the lowest shelf.

● If chicken is not being cooked the same day, remove from packages, wrap loosely in waxed paper or plastic wrap and store on clean plate.

● Make sure liquid from chicken does not drip onto other foods, especially those consumed raw.

● Store whole chicken or chicken pieces for 2 to 3 days, ground chicken for 1 day.

Saucy Chardonnay Chicken ▶

Bathed in a creamy
wine sauce, this elegant
but easy dish is perfect
for entertaining.

3 tbsp	all-purpose flour	50 mL
1/4 tsp	salt	1 mL
Pinch	pepper	Pinch
6	boneless skinless chicken breasts	6
2 tbsp	each butter and olive oil	25 mL
1 cup	Chardonnay wine	250 mL
2	leeks (white and pale green parts), sliced	2
1-1/2 cups	sliced mushrooms	375 mL
1/4 tsp	dried thyme	1 mL
1/2 cup	chicken stock	125 mL
1/2 cup	whipping cream	125 mL
	Chopped fresh parsley	

● In shallow dish, combine 2 tbsp (25 mL) of the flour and half of the salt and pepper; lightly dredge chicken in mixture.

● In large skillet, heat half of the butter and oil over medium-high heat; cook chicken, turning once, for 6 to 8 minutes or until golden brown.

● Add 1/4 cup (50 mL) of the wine to skillet and reduce heat to medium-low; cover and cook for 3 to 4 minutes or until chicken is no longer pink inside. Transfer chicken to warmed serving platter and keep warm; reserve juices separately.

● Add remaining butter and oil to skillet; cook leeks, stirring occasionally, for 5 minutes. Stir in mushrooms and thyme; increase heat to medium and cook, stirring, for 3 minutes. Sprinkle with remaining flour; cook, stirring, for 1 minute.

● Add stock, reserved juices and remaining wine; bring to boil, stirring to scrape up brown bits from bottom of skillet.

● Stir in cream and return to boil; cook, stirring occasionally, for 3 to 4 minutes or until thick enough to coat spoon. Season with remaining salt and pepper. Pour over chicken. Sprinkle with parsley. Makes 6 servings.

TIP: No Chardonnay? You can still make a mean chicken-in-wine sauce with other dry fruity white wines.

Curried Chicken with Mango Chutney

It's forks only for this chunky chicken dish, making it a perfect candidate for buffets. You can double and triple the recipe, make it ahead of time and freeze it, too. Depending on the chutney, you may not need to thicken the sauce with cornstarch.

8	boneless skinless chicken breasts	8
3 tbsp	vegetable oil	50 mL
1	large onion, chopped	1
3	cloves garlic, minced	3
2 tbsp	minced gingerroot	25 mL
1 tbsp	curry powder	15 mL
2 cups	chicken stock	500 mL
1/2 cup	unsweetened desiccated coconut	125 mL
1/2 cup	mango chutney	125 mL
1 tbsp	tomato paste	15 mL
1 tbsp	lemon juice	15 mL
Pinch	each salt and pepper	Pinch
4 tsp	cornstarch	20 mL
4 tsp	water	20 mL

● Cut chicken into 1-inch (2.5 cm) cubes; set aside.

● In skillet, heat oil over medium-high heat; cook onion, garlic, ginger and curry powder for 2 minutes or until onion is softened. Add chicken and stir to coat.

● Mix in stock, coconut, chutney and tomato paste; bring to boil. Reduce heat to medium-low and simmer for 5 minutes. Add lemon juice, salt and pepper; simmer for 4 minutes or until chicken is no longer pink inside.

● Dissolve cornstarch in water; stir into skillet and bring to boil. Reduce heat to medium-low and simmer for about 1 minute or until thickened. Makes 8 servings.

Chicken Goulash ▲

*E*ntertaining on a budget?
*The spicy blend of caraway,
paprika and chili powder in
this goulash puts economical
chicken into a party mood.*

16	chicken thighs	16
3	onions, sliced	3
2	cloves garlic, minced	2
4	carrots, sliced	4
2	sweet green peppers, chopped	2
3 tbsp	sweet Hungarian paprika	50 mL
1 tsp	each caraway seeds and salt	5 mL
1/2 tsp	pepper	2 mL
1/4 tsp	chili powder	1 mL
1 cup	chicken stock	250 mL
1	can (10 oz/284 mL) stewed tomatoes	1
1/2 cup	sour cream	125 mL
2 tbsp	all-purpose flour	25 mL
2 tbsp	chopped fresh parsley	25 mL

● Remove skin from chicken. In Dutch oven, brown chicken over medium-high heat, in batches, until golden. Remove from pan and set aside.

● Drain off fat from pan. Add onions and garlic; cook over medium heat, stirring, for 5 minutes. Add carrots, green peppers, paprika, caraway, salt, pepper and chili powder; cook, stirring, for 2 minutes. Add chicken stock and tomatoes, stirring to scrape up brown bits.

● Return chicken to pan. Bring to boil; reduce heat and simmer for 40 minutes or until chicken is no longer pink inside. Remove to platter; cover and keep warm.

● In small bowl, combine sour cream and flour until smooth. Stir into pan; simmer, stirring, until thickened. Pour over chicken. Garnish with parsley. Makes 8 servings.

Chicken Burritos with Coriander Pesto

3/4 cup	Italian vinaigrette	175 mL
4	boneless skinless chicken breasts	4
4 cups	shredded lettuce	1 L
6	green onions, sliced	6
1 cup	sliced radishes	250 mL
2	large tomatoes, diced	2
1	avocado, peeled and sliced	1
12	flour tortillas, warmed	12
	Coriander Pesto (recipe follows)	

● In flameproof baking dish, pour vinaigrette over chicken; cover and marinate in refrigerator for at least 12 hours or up to 24 hours. Let stand at room temperature for 30 minutes.

● In same dish, broil chicken 4 inches (10 cm) from heat for 10 minutes on each side or until no longer pink inside. Let stand for 10 minutes; slice into thin strips.

● Fill tortillas with lettuce, onions, radishes, tomatoes, avocado and chicken. Drizzle with Coriander Pesto and roll up. Makes 6 servings.

CORIANDER PESTO		
1/4 cup	slivered almonds	50 mL
1/2 tsp	salt	2 mL
1	clove garlic	1
1/2 cup	each packed fresh coriander and parsley	125 mL
2 tbsp	cider vinegar	25 mL
1/2 tsp	each chili powder and granulated sugar	2 mL
1/2 cup	olive oil	125 mL

● In food processor, chop almonds, salt and garlic until fine. Add coriander and parsley; mince. Add vinegar, chili powder and sugar; mix well. With motor running, drizzle in oil. Makes 3/4 cup (175 mL).

Here's a relaxing supper dish that gets everyone around the table filling, drizzling and rolling. And what good tastes and textures plump out a soft-wheat tortilla — grilled chicken, crisp vegetables and a fresh-tasting coriander dressing.

Chilean Chicken and Corn Pie

1 tbsp	vegetable oil	15 mL
2	sweet green peppers, chopped	2
1	large onion, chopped	1
2	cloves garlic, minced	2
1/2 tsp	each cinnamon, chili powder, dried thyme and basil	2 mL
1/2 tsp	each granulated sugar, salt and pepper	2 mL
1/3 cup	raisins	75 mL
1	can (14 oz/398 mL) stewed tomatoes	1
2-1/2 cups	cubed cooked chicken	625 mL
1/2 cup	sliced black olives	125 mL
1-1/2 cups	diced Monterey Jack cheese (8 oz/250 g)	375 mL
	TOPPING	
1	can (14 oz/398 mL) creamed corn	1
1 cup	all-purpose flour	250 mL
1/2 cup	milk	125 mL
1	egg, beaten	1
2 tbsp	butter, melted	25 mL
2 tsp	baking powder	10 mL
Pinch	salt	Pinch

● In skillet, heat oil over medium heat; cook peppers, onion and garlic for 5 minutes. Add cinnamon, chili powder, thyme, basil, sugar, salt and pepper; cook for 1 minute. Add raisins and tomatoes; cook for 5 minutes or until thickened.

● Stir in chicken and olives; remove from heat. Stir in cheese; spread in greased 11- x 7-inch (2 L) baking dish.

● TOPPING: In bowl, combine corn, flour, milk, egg, butter, baking powder and salt; pour evenly over filling. Bake in 400°F (200°C) oven for 35 to 40 minutes or until puffy and golden. Let stand for 10 minutes. Makes 6 servings.

Spoon into the custardy corn bread topping and discover an aromatic chicken, vegetable and cheese filling.

Glorious Roasts

Food fashions come and go but roast chicken never goes out of style. Browning and sputtering in the oven, this simplest of all chickens puts out irresistible aromas that draw everyone eagerly to the dinner table.

Excellent Roast Capon ▶

If a capon is not available, a large roasting chicken is a tasty stand-in. For real old-fashioned Sunday-dinner flavor, be sure to make the Fruit and Bread Dressing (below) to roast alongside.

1	capon (about 8 lb/3.5 kg)	1
Half	lemon	Half
	Salt and pepper	
1	onion, quartered	1
1 tbsp	butter, softened	15 mL
1 tbsp	Dijon mustard	15 mL

● Remove giblets and neck from capon. Rinse and pat capon dry inside and out; rub inside and out with lemon. Sprinkle inside and out with salt and pepper. Place onion in cavity. Tie legs together with string; tuck wings under back. Place, breast side up, on rack in roasting pan.

● Combine butter and mustard; spread over capon. Roast in 325°F (160°C) oven for 2-1/2 hours or until juices run clear when capon is pierced and meat thermometer inserted in thigh registers 185°F (85°C).

● Transfer capon to platter; tent with foil and let stand for about 15 minutes before carving. Makes about 10 servings.

Fruit and Bread Dressing ▶

Onions, apples and herbs make this dressing deliciously moist. Because these flavors are so universal, you can also stuff pork shoulders or loins with this mixture.

1/2 cup	coarsely chopped pitted prunes	125 mL
1/2 cup	chicken stock	125 mL
2 tbsp	butter	25 mL
1	apple, peeled and diced	1
1	stalk celery, chopped	1
6 cups	bread cubes	1.5 L
4	green onions, sliced	4
2 tbsp	chopped fresh parsley	25 mL
1/4 tsp	each dried thyme and sage	1 mL
	Salt and pepper	
2 tbsp	pan drippings or melted butter	25 mL

● Soak prunes in chicken stock. Meanwhile, in large skillet, melt butter over medium heat; cook apple and celery, stirring often, for 5 minutes. Remove from heat.

● Stir in bread cubes, prunes with stock, green onions, parsley, thyme, sage, and salt and pepper to taste.

● Transfer to 8-cup (2 L) casserole; drizzle with pan drippings. Cover and bake in 325°F (160°C) oven for 30 minutes or until heated through. Makes 10 servings.

TIP: For a crisp crust on top of the dressing, uncover and bake for about 10 minutes longer than called for in the recipe.

ROASTING CHICKEN

When buying a roasting chicken, look for plump, dry-skinned chickens. Good roasters vary in size from 3-1/2 to 6 lb (1.6 to 2.7 kg), and any of the recipes in this chapter can be made with chickens in this size range. The smaller chickens serve four or five, while the larger ones are feasts for up to eight. *Canadian Living's* Test Kitchen recommends roasting chickens at 325°F (160°C) for 20 to 30 minutes per pound (500 g).

Classic Roast Chicken

Roast chicken lends itself to so many colorful variations — with herbs, with spices, with coatings and stuffings. But why not start off with the vanilla of chickens — a good plain roast.

1	chicken (3-1/2 lb/1.75 kg)	1
1	clove garlic	1
2	sprigs fresh thyme	2
1	carrot, halved	1
Half	onion, quartered	Half
1 tbsp	butter	15 mL
1 tsp	dried thyme	5 mL
1/4 tsp	each salt and pepper	1 mL
1-1/2 cups	chicken stock	375 mL
1/2 cup	dry white wine	125 mL
1-1/2 tsp	all-purpose flour	7 mL

● Remove giblets and neck from chicken. Rinse and pat chicken dry inside and out; stuff cavity with thyme sprigs, carrot, onion and garlic. Tie legs together with string; tuck wings under back. Rub butter over chicken; sprinkle with thyme, salt and pepper.

● Place chicken, breast side up, on rack in roasting pan; pour in 1/2 cup (125 mL) of the chicken stock and the wine. Roast in 325°F (160°C) oven, basting every 30 minutes and adding up to 1/2 cup (125 mL) more chicken stock if liquid evaporates, for 1-3/4 to 2 hours or until juices run clear when chicken is pierced and meat thermometer inserted in thigh registers 185°F (85°C).

● Transfer chicken to platter; tent with foil and let stand for 10 minutes before carving.

● Meanwhile, skim fat from pan. Sprinkle flour over pan juices; cook over medium-high heat, stirring, for 1 minute. Pour in remaining 1/2 cup (125 mL) stock. Cook, stirring, until thickened. Pour into warmed gravy boat and serve with chicken. Makes 4 to 5 servings.

Prairie Roast Chicken

1	chicken (3-1/2 lb/1.75 kg)	1
1/3 cup	Dijon mustard	75 mL
2 tsp	soy sauce	10 mL
1 tsp	minced gingerroot	5 mL
1	clove garlic, minced	1
2 cups	chicken stock	500 mL
4 tsp	all-purpose flour	20 m

● Remove giblets and neck from chicken. Rinse and pat chicken dry inside and out. Tie legs together with string; tuck wings under back. Place, breast side up, on rack in roasting pan.

● Combine mustard, soy sauce, ginger and garlic; brush all over chicken. Pour in 1-1/2 cups (375 mL) of the chicken stock. Roast in 325°F (160°C) oven, basting every 30 minutes, for 1-3/4 to 2 hours or until juices run clear when chicken is pierced and meat thermometer inserted in thigh registers 185°F (85°C).

● Transfer chicken to platter; tent with foil and let stand for 10 minutes before carving.

● Meanwhile, skim fat from pan. Sprinkle flour over pan juices; cook over medium-high heat, stirring, for 1 minute. Pour in remaining chicken stock; cook, stirring, until thickened. Pour into warmed gravy boat and serve with chicken. Makes 4 to 5 servings.

In France, they might call this mustardy chicken "dijonnaise," ascribing the mustard's origins to the Burgundian city of Dijon. However, while the good citizens of Dijon ground and blended the mustard, the good citizens of the Prairies grew the mustard seeds. So to these hardy mustard producers goes the name — with thanks.

Roast Chicken with Garlic Gravy

1	chicken (3-1/2 lb/1.75 kg)	1
10	cloves garlic, peeled	10
1 tsp	dried thyme	5 mL
1/4 tsp	each salt and pepper	1 mL
1-1/4 cups	chicken stock	300 mL
1/2 cup	white wine or chicken stock	125 mL
1 tbsp	all-purpose flour	15 mL

● Remove giblets and neck from chicken. Rinse and pat chicken dry inside and out. Place 2 garlic cloves in cavity. Starting at cavity opening, gently lift skin and rub thyme, salt and pepper over breasts and legs. Tie legs together with string; tuck wings under back.

● Add remaining garlic, half of the chicken stock and the wine to roasting pan; place chicken, breast side up, on rack in pan. Roast in 325°F (160°C) oven, basting every 30 minutes and adding additional stock if pan juices evaporate, for 1-3/4 to 2 hours or until juices run clear when chicken is pierced and meat thermometer inserted in thigh registers 185°F (85°C).

● Transfer to platter; tent with foil and let stand for 10 minutes before carving.

● Meanwhile, strain pan juices into measure, pressing down firmly to mash garlic into juices; skim off fat. Add enough of the remaining stock to make 3/4 cup (175 mL).

● In small saucepan, stir together 2 tbsp (25 mL) of the pan juices and flour; cook, stirring, over medium heat for 1 minute. Gradually whisk in remaining pan juices; cook, stirring, until boiling and thickened. Serve with chicken. Makes 4 to 5 servings.

Whole garlic buds, roasted with the chicken, add a deliciously mellow flavor to the lightened-up gravy.

TIP: Rub flavorings such as herbs and spices under the skin. Roast the chicken, remove the skin and enjoy the flavors roasted into the succulent meat.

Lemon Chicken with Mashed Potatoes ▼

A romatic seasonings and simple styling turn traditional roast chicken and mashed potatoes into a new dish that looks, smells and tastes wonderful. Serve with green beans and garnish the plates with lemon slices.

1	chicken (4 lb/1.8 kg)	1
	Salt and pepper	
1	lemon, peeled and sliced	1
2	cloves garlic	2
1 tbsp	dried rosemary	15 mL
1 tbsp	olive oil	15 mL
1 tsp	fennel seeds	5 mL
1/2 cup	chicken stock	125 mL
1 tsp	soy sauce	5 mL
1 tsp	tomato paste	5 mL

	POTATOES	
4	large baking potatoes, peeled and quartered	4
2 tbsp	olive oil	25 mL
1	small clove garlic, minced	1
Pinch	ground cumin	Pinch
1/2 tsp	each salt and pepper	2 mL
	Chopped fresh parsley	

● Remove giblets and neck from chicken. Rinse and pat chicken dry inside and out; sprinkle inside and out with salt and pepper. Stuff with lemon, garlic and rosemary. Tie legs together with string; tuck wings under back. Brush with oil; sprinkle with fennel seeds.

● Place chicken, breast side up, on rack in roasting pan. Roast in 325°F (160°C) oven for 2 to 2-1/4 hours or until juices run clear when chicken is pierced and meat thermometer inserted in thigh registers 185°F (85°C).

● Transfer chicken to platter; spoon juices from cavity into roasting pan and stir to mix with pan juices. Tent chicken with foil; let stand for 10 minutes before cutting into serving-size pieces.

● Meanwhile, stir chicken stock into pan juices; bring to boil, stirring to scrape up brown bits. Boil for about 5 minutes or until reduced by one-quarter. Strain and skim off fat. Whisk in soy sauce, tomato paste, and salt to taste.

● POTATOES: Meanwhile, in saucepan of boiling salted water, cook potatoes for about 20 minutes or until tender; drain and mash. Mix in oil, garlic, cumin, salt and pepper.

● On each of 4 warmed plates, mound potatoes; pool sauce around potatoes. Place chicken alongside; sprinkle with parsley. Makes 4 servings.

Prosciutto Roasted Chicken

1	chicken (3-1/2 lb/1.75 kg)	1
4	slices prosciutto, chopped	4
4 tsp	chopped fresh sage	20 mL
1	clove garlic, minced	1
2 tsp	olive oil	10 mL
2 cups	chicken stock	500 mL
1 tbsp	balsamic vinegar	15 mL
2 tsp	all-purpose flour	10 mL

● Remove giblets and neck from chicken. Rinse and pat chicken dry inside and out. Using fingers, gently loosen skin from chicken breasts and legs to form pockets, leaving skin attached at edges.

● Combine prosciutto, 1 tbsp (15 mL) of the sage and the garlic; stuff into each pocket, patting gently to spread and flatten slightly.

● Tie legs together with string; tuck wings under back. Rub oil over chicken; sprinkle with remaining sage.

● Place chicken, breast side up, on rack in roasting pan. Pour in 1-1/2 cups (375 mL) of the chicken stock and vinegar. Roast in 325°F (160°C) oven, basting every 30 minutes, for 1-3/4 to 2 hours or until juices run clear when chicken is pierced and meat thermometer inserted in thigh registers 185°F (85°C).

● Transfer chicken to platter; tent with foil and let stand for 10 minutes before carving.

● Meanwhile, skim fat from pan. Sprinkle flour over pan juices; cook over medium-high heat, stirring, for 1 minute. Pour in remaining chicken stock; cook, stirring, until thickened. Pour into warmed gravy boat and serve with chicken. Makes 4 to 5 servings.

Prosciutto, cured unsmoked ham, marks this recipe as Italian-inspired. And while we don't often think of sage as Italian, it is, in fact, found often in northern Italian cooking and joins up pleasingly with the prosciutto and balsamic vinegar.

HOW TO CARVE A ROAST CHICKEN

Carving is a practical skill that will show off the chicken you have roasted in its most beautiful way. Make sure the serving platter is well warmed and the gravy that goes alongside is piping hot.

Large Roaster

1 Place chicken, breast side up, on cutting board. Point legs right if you are right-handed, left if you are left-handed. Remove skewers or string.

2 Gently pull leg away from body while cutting through joint that holds leg to body. Place leg, meaty side up, on cutting board and cut through joint to separate drumstick from thigh. Repeat with second leg. Arrange legs on heated platter and cover to keep warm.

3 Gently pull wing away from body while cutting through joint holding it to body. Repeat with other wing and add to platter.

4 Steady bird by inserting long-pronged fork into ridge at top of breast. With sharp knife, cut slices parallel to side of chicken. Start about halfway up side in order to divide up the succulent skin equally. Overlap slices attractively on platter. Repeat with other side.

Small Bird

1 Place chicken on cutting board and steady with a long-pronged fork.

2 Using poultry or kitchen shears or a sharp knife, cut chicken into quarters — two breast portions and two leg portions. For more than four portions, cut each leg at joint to make drumstick and thigh pieces.

Roast Chicken with Greek Touches

Oregano, mint, garlic and lemon bathe both chicken and potatoes in sunny Mediterranean flavors.

6	baking potatoes	6
1	chicken (4 lb/1.8 kg)	1
3 tbsp	olive oil	50 mL
3 tbsp	lemon juice	50 mL
2 tsp	dried oregano	10 mL
2 tsp	dried mint	10 mL
6	large cloves garlic, coarsely slivered	6
1 cup	chicken stock	250 mL

● Peel potatoes and cut into eighths; place in saucepan and cover with cold water. Bring to boil; boil for 10 minutes. Drain.

● Remove giblets and neck from chicken. Rinse and pat chicken dry inside and out. Tie legs together with string; tuck wings under back. Place, breast side up, on rack in roasting pan.

● Rub 1 tbsp (15 mL) each of the olive oil and lemon juice all over chicken; sprinkle with 1 tsp (5 mL) each of the oregano and mint.

● Arrange potatoes and garlic around chicken. Drizzle remaining oil and lemon juice over potatoes; sprinkle potatoes with remaining oregano and mint. Pour in chicken stock.

● Roast in 325°F (160°C) oven, basting chicken and potatoes every 30 minutes, for 2 to 2-1/4 hours or until juices run clear when chicken is pierced and meat thermometer inserted in thigh registers 185°F (85°C).

● Transfer chicken to platter; tent with foil and let stand for 10 minutes before carving. Serve with potatoes and skimmed pan juices. Makes 5 to 6 servings.

Moroccan Roast Chicken ▶

This succulent chicken is fragrant with spices you'll find in your cupboard — plus lemons, onions, prunes and green olives that give it an authentic, pleasingly exotic taste. Accompany with couscous, green beans and glazed carrots.

1	chicken (5 lb/2.2 kg)	1
2	lemons, sliced	2
1	large onion, sliced	1
1/3 cup	butter, softened	75 mL
2	cloves garlic, minced	2
2 tbsp	grated gingerroot	25 mL
1/2 tsp	each cinnamon, allspice, paprika and salt	2 mL
1/2 tsp	each ground cumin and cloves	2 mL
1 cup	dried prunes	250 mL
1 cup	large pitted green olives, halved lengthwise	250 mL

● Remove giblets and neck from chicken. Rinse and pat chicken dry inside and out; stuff cavity with half of the lemons. Arrange remaining lemons and onion in roasting pan. Tie legs together with string; tuck neck flap under bird. Place, breast side up, on rack over onion and lemons in pan.

● Combine butter, garlic, ginger, cinnamon, allspice, paprika, salt, cumin and cloves; spread over chicken. Add prunes, olives and 1 cup (250 mL) water to pan.

● Roast in 325°F (160°C) oven, basting every 20 minutes, for about 2-1/4 hours or until juices run clear when chicken is pierced and meat thermometer inserted in thigh registers 185°F (85°C).

● Remove to platter; surround with olives and prunes. Tent with foil and let stand for 10 minutes before carving. Skim off fat from pan juices; serve juices with chicken. Makes 7 to 8 servings.

Sweetly Spicy Chicken with Couscous Stuffing

Couscous is a new and impressive twist for stuffing chicken. Almonds and currants make the dish festive and complement the sweet spices coating the chicken.

2 tbsp	butter	25 mL
4	green onions, chopped	4
1	clove garlic, minced	1
1-1/2 tsp	ground cumin	7 mL
1/2 tsp	each dried coriander and ground ginger	2 mL
Pinch	each cinnamon, salt and pepper	Pinch
3-1/2 cups	chicken stock	875 mL
1 cup	couscous	250 mL
1/4 cup	currants	50 mL
1/4 cup	chopped almonds	50 mL
3 tbsp	chopped fresh parsley	45 mL
1	chicken (4 lb/1.8 kg)	1
1/4 tsp	curry powder	1 mL
1 tbsp	liquid honey (optional)	15 mL
4 tsp	all-purpose flour	20 mL

● In saucepan, melt 1 tbsp (15 mL) of the butter over medium heat; cook onions and garlic, stirring, for 3 minutes or until softened. Stir in 1/2 tsp (2 mL) of the cumin, 1/4 tsp (1 mL) each of the coriander and ginger, the cinnamon, salt and pepper; cook, stirring, for 1 minute.

● Pour in 1-1/2 cups (375 mL) of the chicken stock; bring to boil. Stir in couscous, currants, almonds and parsley; remove from heat. Cover and let stand for 5 minutes; fluff with fork.

● Remove giblets and neck from chicken. Rinse and pat chicken dry inside and out. Stuff cavity with half of the couscous mixture; place remaining couscous in ovenproof serving dish. Tie legs together with string; tuck wings under back. Place, breast side up, on rack in roasting pan.

● Combine remaining cumin, coriander, ginger and the curry powder; sprinkle over chicken. Pour in 1-1/2 cups (375 mL) of the remaining chicken stock.

● Roast in 325°F (160°C) oven, basting every 30 minutes, for 1-1/2 hours. Brush with honey (if using); place dish of couscous in oven. Roast for about 30 minutes longer or until juices run clear when chicken is pierced and meat thermometer inserted in thigh registers 185°F (85°C).

● Transfer chicken to platter; tent with foil and let stand for 10 minutes before carving.

● Meanwhile, skim fat from pan. Sprinkle flour over pan juices; cook over medium-high heat, stirring, for 1 minute. Pour in remaining chicken stock; cook, stirring, until thickened. Pour into warmed gravy boat and serve with chicken and stuffing. Makes 5 to 6 servings.

HOW TO STUFF A CHICKEN

1 Always stuff chicken just before cooking. Rinse the neck and body cavities and pat dry.

2 Prepare about 3/4 cup (175 mL) stuffing per pound (500 g) of chicken.

If stuffing does not contain meat, have it at room temperature.

3 Fill the neck cavity (wishbone area) first, spooning in stuffing until full but not bulging or compacted.

4 Pull the neck skin to the back of the chicken and fasten with metal skewer. Fill the body cavity, again without packing.

5 Any extra stuffing can be placed in a covered casserole or heavy foil, drizzled with pan drippings if desired, and baked alongside chicken for the last 30 to 45 minutes of roasting time or until heated through.

Hoisin Glazed Roast Chicken

1	chicken (3-1/2 lb/1.75 kg)	1
2 tbsp	hoisin sauce	25 mL
1 tbsp	minced gingerroot	15 mL
1 tbsp	liquid honey	15 mL
1 tbsp	soy sauce	15 mL
1/4 tsp	sesame oil	1 mL
2	cloves garlic, minced	2
2 cups	chicken stock	500 mL
4 tsp	all-purpose flour	20 mL

● Remove giblets and neck from chicken. Rinse and pat chicken dry inside and out. Tie legs together with string; tuck wings under back. Place, breast side up, on rack in roasting pan.

● Combine hoisin sauce, ginger, honey, soy sauce, sesame oil and garlic; brush over chicken. Pour 1-1/2 cups (375 mL) of the chicken stock into pan. Roast in 325°F (160°C) oven, basting every 30 minutes, for 1-3/4 to 2 hours or until juices run clear when chicken is pierced and meat thermometer inserted in thigh registers 185°F (85°C).

● Transfer chicken to platter; tent with foil and let stand for 10 minutes before carving.

● Meanwhile, skim fat from pan; sprinkle flour over pan juices. Cook over medium-high heat, stirring, for 1 minute. Pour in remaining chicken stock; cook, stirring, until thickened. Pour into warmed gravy boat and serve with chicken. Makes 4 to 5 servings.

The Oriental flavors suggest rice and steamed greens as side dishes. Choose sugar snap peas, asparagus, bok choy or broccoli.

TIP: Hoisin sauce — a mixture of soybeans, garlic, hot peppers and spices — is an increasingly popular flavor, especially for stir-fries and for glazing roasted meats and poultry. Look for it in Chinese grocery stores and in supermarkets that stock Oriental ingredients. Once opened, store jar in the refrigerator.

Tarragon Lemon Chicken

1	chicken (3-1/2 lb/1.75 kg)	1
1	lemon, halved	1
1/4 cup	butter, softened	50 mL
2 tbsp	chopped fresh tarragon	25 mL
1/2 tsp	grated lemon rind	2 mL
2 cups	chicken stock	500 mL
1 tbsp	lemon juice	15 mL
4 tsp	all-purpose flour	20 mL

● Remove giblets and neck from chicken. Rinse and pat chicken dry inside and out. Place lemon in cavity. Using fingers, gently loosen skin from chicken breasts and legs to form pockets, leaving skin attached at edges.

● Combine butter, tarragon and lemon rind; stuff into each pocket, patting gently to spread and flatten slightly. Tie legs together with string; tuck wings under back.

● Place chicken, breast side up, on rack in roasting pan. Pour in 1-1/2 cups (375 mL) of the chicken stock and the lemon juice. Roast in 325°F (160°C) oven, basting every 30 minutes, for 1-3/4 to 2 hours or until juices run clear when chicken is pierced and meat thermometer inserted in thigh registers 185°F (85°C).

● Transfer chicken to platter; tent with foil and let stand for 10 minutes before carving.

● Meanwhile, skim fat from pan. Sprinkle flour over pan juices; cook, stirring, for 1 minute. Pour in remaining chicken stock; cook, stirring, until thickened. Pour into warmed gravy boat and serve with chicken. Makes 4 to 5 servings.

Tarragon has a delicate licorice flavor that enhances chicken without taking over. Pushing the stuffing under the skin puts the flavor where it counts.

Chicken and Corn Medley ▶

This is a welcome dinner for weeknights or weekends. The chicken, cut in half for speedier roasting, tends itself while the harvest vegetables simmer. Offer warmed tortillas or crusty sourdough bread alongside.

1	chicken (4 lb/1.8 kg), halved (see p. 64)	1
1 tsp	vegetable oil	5 mL
2 tsp	paprika	10 mL
3/4 tsp	pepper	4 mL
1/2 tsp	salt	2 mL
1/2 tsp	each dried oregano and dry mustard	2 mL
Pinch	hot pepper flakes	Pinch
	CORN MEDLEY	
2 tsp	vegetable oil	10 mL
1	onion, chopped	1
2	cloves garlic, minced	2
2	tomatoes, chopped	2
1	zucchini, finely chopped	1
1/2 tsp	each paprika, chili powder and salt	2 mL
1/4 tsp	each dried oregano and ground cumin	1 mL
1/4 tsp	pepper	1 mL
1	sweet red or green pepper, chopped	1
3 cups	corn niblets	750 mL
1 tbsp	lime juice	15 mL
	Lime wedges	

● Place chicken halves, skin side up, on rimmed baking sheet; brush with oil. Combine paprika, pepper, salt, oregano, mustard and hot pepper flakes; sprinkle evenly over chicken. Let stand at room temperature for 30 minutes.

● Roast in 375°F (190°C) oven for about 1 hour or until juices run clear when chicken is pierced with fork.

● CORN MEDLEY: Meanwhile, in nonstick skillet, heat oil over medium heat; cook onion and garlic, stirring, for 1 minute. Stir in tomatoes, zucchini, paprika, chili powder, salt, oregano, cumin and pepper; cook, stirring occasionally, for about 8 minutes or until most of the liquid has evaporated. Stir in red pepper, corn and lime juice; cook, stirring, for about 5 minutes or until vegetables are tender.

● Spoon vegetables onto warmed serving platter; arrange chicken on top. Garnish with lime wedges. Makes 5 to 6 servings.

Coriander Roast Chicken

While coriander is the herb of choice here, fresh basil is a robust alternative. Depending on your mood, round out the menu with Basmati rice and glazed carrots — or mashed sweet potatoes and crunchy green beans.

1	chicken (3-1/2 lb/1.75 kg)	1
Half	lemon	Half
1/3 cup	chopped fresh coriander	75 mL
1	clove garlic, minced	1
4 tsp	olive oil	20 mL
1/4 tsp	each salt and pepper	1 mL

● Remove giblets and neck from chicken. Rinse and pat chicken dry inside and out. Place lemon in cavity. Using fingers, gently loosen skin from chicken breasts and legs to form pockets, leaving skin attached at edges.

● Combine coriander and garlic; stuff into each pocket, patting gently to flatten slightly. Tie legs together with string; tuck wings under back. Rub oil over chicken; sprinkle with salt and pepper.

● Place chicken, breast side up, on rack in roasting pan. Roast in 325°F (160°C) oven for 1-3/4 to 2 hours or until juices run clear when chicken is pierced and meat thermometer inserted in thigh registers 185°F (85°C).

● Transfer chicken to platter; tent with foil and let stand for 10 minutes before carving. Makes 4 to 5 servings.

The Contributors

Photography Credits

FRED BIRD:
front and back covers,
copyright page, pages 7,
11, 12, 15, 16, 19, 21, 23,
25, 26, 27, 29, 31, 32, 35,
37, 38, 41, 45, 49, 50, 52,
54, 56, 58, 61, 62, 65, 67,
71, 75, 76, 79, 80, 82, 85,
89, 96.

CHRISTOPHER
CAMPBELL:
page 8.

JOHN SHERLOCK:
page 68.

CURTIS TRENT:
front flap.

BOB WIGINGTON:
page 4.

Special Thanks

Acknowledging the people who have made *Canadian Living's Best Chicken* is a pleasure. The creativity, meticulous eye and organizing skills of Madison Press project editor Wanda Nowakowska are first in line for appreciation, as are Beverley Renahan, *Canadian Living* senior editor, and Daphna Rabinovitch, manager of *Canadian Living's* Test Kitchen. Others at the magazine are due sincere thanks as well: Test Kitchen staff shown on the front flap, plus Vicki Burns, Janet Cornish and Christine Levac, and senior editor Donna Paris. Our "looks good enough to eat" photography comes largely via the skills of creative director Deborah Fadden, food stylists Jennifer McLagan and Olga Truchan, and photographer Fred Bird, and the clean user-friendly design from Gord Sibley. Dinners across Canada are all the tastier because of the contributions of *Canadian Living's* very accomplished food writers, the finest in the land. Of course, all of our work at *Canadian Living* is under the guidance of editor-in-chief Bonnie Cowan and publisher Kirk Shearer, whose commitment to *The Best* series is wonderful encouragement.

Elizabeth Baird

Index

EDITORIAL DIRECTOR
Hugh Brewster

PROJECT EDITOR
Wanda Nowakowska

EDITORIAL ASSISTANCE
Beverley Renahan

PRODUCTION DIRECTOR
Susan Barrable

PRODUCTION COORDINATOR
Donna Chong

BOOK DESIGN AND LAYOUT
Gordon Sibley Design Inc.

COLOR SEPARATION
Colour Technologies

PRINTING AND BINDING
Friesen Printers

CANADIAN LIVING ADVISORY BOARD
Robert A. Murray, Kirk Shearer, Caren King,
Bonnie Baker Cowan, Elizabeth Baird, Anna Hobbs

CANADIAN LIVING'S™ BEST CHICKEN
was produced by Madison Press Books
under the direction of Albert E. Cummings